YORK NOTES

General Editors: Professor A.N. Jeffares (*Univ*
of Stirling) & Professor Suheil Bushrui (*America*
University of Beirut)

ish play is to be studied or

Tennessee Williams

A STREETCAR
NAMED DESIRE

Notes by Hana Sambrook

MA, PH D (EDINBURGH)

LONGMAN
YORK PRESS

THE LEARNING CENTRE
TOWER HAMLETS COLLEGE
POPLAR CENTRE
POPLAR HIGH STREET
LONDON E14 0AF

YORK PRESS
Immeuble Esseily, Place Riad Solh, Beirut

ADDISON WESLEY LONGMAN LIMITED
Edinburgh Gate, Harlow
Essex CM20 2JE, England
Associated companies, branches and representatives
throughout the world

First published 1995
Fourth impression 1997

ISBN 0–582–26245–3

Phototypeset by Gem Graphics, Trenance, Mawgan Porth, Cornwall
Printed in Singapore

Contents

Contents

Part 1

Introduction

The life of Tennessee Williams

Strangely, Tennessee Williams came not from Tennessee, but from Columbus, Mississippi. His grandfather, the Rev. Walter E. Dakin was the rector of the Columbus Episcopal church, and he and his wife were highly respected members of local society. They had one child, Edwina, who grew up into a typical Southern belle, pretty, spoilt and hopeless in domestic matters, having been brought up to rely on black servants.

In 1907 Edwina married Cornelius Coffin Williams, then an employee of a telephone company. He was well connected on both his parents' sides (his father's family had Huguenot links), and altogether he was regarded as a highly suitable match for the Dakins' only child. The Williamses first had a little girl, Rose, and then, two years later, on 26 March 1911 Mrs Williams gave birth to a boy, christened Thomas Lanier (after a Huguenot ancestor). The nickname 'Tennessee' came much later, having been given to Williams by his fellow students at college who confused one Southern state, Tennessee, with another, Mississippi. To his family Williams was always known as Tom.

Although there was a third child, a boy, Walter Dakin, born eight years after Williams, the two elder children were utterly devoted to each other and happiest when alone together. When Williams was seven years old he fell dangerously ill with diphtheria and his illness and long convalescence kept him at home while his mother nursed him back into health. In this way circumstances served to forge even closer links between Williams, his sister and his mother. Later he came to regret and even resent the closeness of these family ties. In general, however, the two children had a happy childhood, living with their mother mostly in their maternal grandparents' rectory. Right from the earliest days the Williamses' marriage seems not to have been very happy. Cornelius Williams's job kept him away from home much of the time and his wife and children grew to prefer the security and comfort of the rectory. Mrs Williams especially was delighted to share her parents' established position as pillars of society in a series of small Southern towns, always in Mississippi. She delighted in the respect of the townspeople, and developed the rather commanding, autocratic manner of a Southern lady. Her supreme self-confidence served her well over the years, sheltering her from any unpleasant reality.

In 1918 Cornelius Williams found a new job as manager of a shoe company in St Louis. For the children the move to St Louis meant the loss of a familiar background and of their grandparents' loving care. Meanwhile their mother now found herself deprived of her assured social status and commanding position in a small town. She had her third child, Dakin, at this time, and two years later she miscarried her fourth and last child.

The move to St Louis, with its attendant miseries, seems to have exacerbated the disagreements between Cornelius and Edwina and from this time onwards the Williams household became a place of strife or silent bitterness. The husband grew moody and began to drink heavily, while his spoilt, impractical wife resented her humdrum life of petty economies. She felt that she had lost her rightful place in society, and blamed her husband for the loss, inviting the children to share her resentment.

To escape from the unhappiness at home, Williams now turned to reading and also to writing. Later in life, he was to draw on these early documents and transform the feelings of misery and suffering he had recorded into the raw material of his plays. Williams was also successful in having his early work published. His high school magazine accepted his poems and stories and he became a regular contributor as a film critic, among other things. This early enthusiasm for the cinema would later become apparent in the style and construction of his plays.

While happy about the success of his attempts at writing, the boy grew more and more miserable about the situation at home. One particular cause of misery was the increasingly strange behaviour of his beloved sister Rose. Her pathological shyness and the fits of intense melancholy to which she became subject were forever a source of anxiety, especially to her mother whose matrimonial plans for Rose were constantly thwarted. Eligible young men were invited to the house but they never seemed to come back for a second visit.

In the summer of 1928 Williams was able to escape this misery temporarily when his grandfather, the Rev. Dakin, arranged a European tour for some members of his congregation. Williams was invited to accompany the party and in their two months away they visited Paris, Monte Carlo, Venice, Milan and Montreux, and saw the castles of the Rhine. For the teenager it was as if a window opened on to a world he had never dreamt of and the experience remained a cherished and inspiring memory for the rest of his life. After he became successful and rich, his visits to Europe remained a regular feature right up to the last weeks of his life.

It was through his grandmother's generosity that, in the following year, he became a student at the University of Missouri, at Columbia. In his three years there he did not distinguish himself academically but did begin to make a name for himself as a writer. He also discovered the great modern dramatists – August Strindberg (1849–1912), Anton Chekhov (1860–1904), Henrik Ibsen (1828–1906).

Then came the Depression, and Williams's academic career was cut short for financial reasons. There followed a miserable period when he worked as a clerk at the International Shoe Company where his father was employed as well. Even during this wretched time he continued to write and get his work published. However, the strain of holding on to his clerical job while continuing to pursue his literary career, combined with the deteriorating situation at home, took its toll on Williams's health. It seems that he suffered some kind of physical collapse and was obliged to move to his grandparents' house (now in Memphis) to recuperate. During his convalescence a play of his, *Cairo, Shanghai, Bombay*, was performed by a local amateur group (1935).

Once he had recovered, and his family's financial position had improved somewhat, he enrolled as a student at Washington University in St Louis. He continued to read voraciously and to write. He also started to gain some recognition at this time and had two short plays (*Candles in the Sun* and *Fugitive Kind*) put on by a small theatre group at the university.

It was during this period of some success for Williams himself that Rose's mental health worsened drastically, and early in 1937 she was committed to a mental hospital after several violent outbursts, directed mostly against her father. Perhaps to distance himself from this unhappiness Williams moved to the University of Iowa. Here his academic work improved and his writing career began to advance rapidly. Here, too, he seems to have come to terms with his homosexuality.

In the autumn of 1937, however, an event took place which must have made his personal problems seem small by comparison. Rose's mental instability now took the form of violent sexual fantasies and she accused her father of attacking her. It was the sexual element in Rose's ravings and the threat of a scandal that finally pushed Mrs Williams into giving her consent for a pre-frontal lobotomy to be performed on her daughter. Williams blamed himself for being absent at this critical time and so permitting the operation to take place. He never forgave himself, nor could he ever forgive his mother for allowing her daughter to be turned into a non-person, at peace, but with no memories, no fears and no mind. His mother, protected by her armour of self-confidence, seems to have been unaware of his feelings and, as a result, the relationship between mother and son changed. From this time onwards Williams became increasingly aware of the destructive nature of some kinds of mother love. He was haunted by his guilt about Rose to the end of his days, and she makes appearances in a number of his plays. She is the obvious inspiration of *The Glass Menagerie*, but there is surely much of here in poor unstable Blanche in *A Streetcar Named Desire* as well: she too was committed to a mental hospital with the connivance of her family. Catherine in *Suddenly Last Summer* is a very different person from Rose, but she only narrowly escapes a similar fate.

For the next two years life was neither easy nor settled for Williams. Though he finally graduated from the University of Iowa in August 1938, his prospects for finding employment were non-existent. He drifted, to Chicago, St Louis, New Orleans, California and Mexico, taking ill-paid manual jobs and trying without success to gain patronage from official sources. Indeed it was his search for official sponsorship that took him to New Orleans, which he found exciting and liberating and which allowed him to express his sexual identity fully for the first time.

At this point he took a bold step which was to change his career. He sent a selection of his short plays, entitled *American Blues*, to the prestigious Group Theatre Play Contest in New York. Though he did not win the Group's prize, he was awarded a $100 special prize (1939) in recognition of his talent. Moreover, Audrey Wood, who ran the best theatre agency of the time, offered to represent him. For years after, she took care of his finances, his contracts, his hopelessly impractical, disorganised life, and remained his staunch friend. With her help he was awarded a Rockefeller writing fellowship and completed a full-length play, *Battle of Angels* (1940), which was staged by the Theatre Guild and proved a respectable failure.

Another period of drifting followed, which included a visit to Frieda Lawrence in Taos, New Mexico. This resulted in a short play, *I Rise in Flames, Cried the Phoenix*, staged much later, in 1958. It is an act of homage to D. H. Lawrence, a writer whose view of sexuality as a vital force was a major influence on Williams. This period of drifting was made particularly painful for him by his much loved grandmother's battle against cancer which was eventually to kill her in 1944. However, Williams was able to help with her medical bills when Audrey Wood obtained for him a lucrative contract as script-writer for the film company Metro-Goldwyn-Mayer in 1943. He produced only one script, entitled *The Gentleman Caller*. That MGM turned it down is unimportant, given that the script became his celebrated play *The Glass Menagerie*. It was written during a period of mourning for his grandmother and is a lament both for his sister Rose and for the misery of his family life. (According to Dakin Williams, the playwright's younger brother, the play is 'a virtually literal rendering' of the Williams family life.)

The play opened in Chicago in December 1944, and in New York the following March, winning two prestigious critical awards. An earlier play, *You Touched Me*, was staged in New York in September 1945. Now a successful, fêted author, free from financial worries at last, Williams left for a holiday in Mexico. There he worked seriously on a new play which he had started in Chicago in spring 1945. Originally entitled *The Moth*, the play was later retitled *Blanche's Chair in the Moon*, and retitled again *The Poker Night*. (Readers of *A Streetcar Named Desire* will recognise the changing emphases of the successive versions of the play.)

Williams was also writing short stories, some of which were later re-worked into his plays. His creative energy was enormous, as was his appetite for life, and he became increasingly promiscuous. Significantly he moved to New Orleans, which for him symbolised artistic and sexual freedom, and he made it the setting for *A Streetcar Named Desire*. Williams was preoccupied with the play for a long time, uncertain how it should develop and what should be Blanche DuBois's fate. The final version was directed by Elia Kazan (who also directed the highly acclaimed 1951 screen version), and it was an instant success, winning the Pulitzer Prize, as well as the New York Drama Critics Circle Award. Undecided about what his next step should be, Williams left for Europe at the end of 1947. He spent some time in Paris and then went on to Italy as if to retrace that wonderful Grand Tour of his youth – though in a rather different spirit. He was working on a new play, *Summer and Smoke*, but it seems that most of his energy went into looking for sexual partners. At about this time he seems to have taken to drugs as well as to alcohol to heighten his pleasures.

He was now a wealthy man, with the screen rights for *The Glass Menagerie* and *A Streetcar Named Desire* adding to the income from his stage plays. He was able to provide for his family, especially for Rose, and it was at this time that he bought the house in Key West, Florida, which was to be his home for much of his later years. Free from financial anxieties he went to Rome once more, to write a novel, *The Roman Spring of Mrs Stone* (published 1950), in which the heroine's hectic search for lovers may be seen as a thinly disguised self-appraisal of the author's own search for male partners.

After *The Roman Spring of Mrs Stone* Williams went back to writing plays with *The Rose Tattoo*, which had its first performance in New York in 1961. It too was turned into a successful film. His life continued with the same mixture of hard work, drinking and pill-taking; in 1953 *Camino Real* had its première in New York with only moderate success. His next play, *Cat on a Hot Tin Roof* (again directed by Elia Kazan), broke new ground for Williams in its density of form (it subscribes to the three unitics of time, space and action, and Williams stresses the first two in his note 'There is no lapse of time' at the beginning of Acts II and III. See p. 42 of these Notes for further discussion on these three unities), as well as in its spirit of tolerance, of common humanity. Williams found it a difficult play to write (he rewrote Act III at Kazan's insistence) and was anxious about its reception. In the midst of these anxieties he received news of his beloved grandfather's death. Jointly with his wife old Mr Dakin gave Williams the love and care the playwright had never had from his parents, and his death was a great loss. *Cat on a Hot Tin Roof* was a resounding success, encouraging Williams to work on the scenario of a new film for Kazan, *Baby Doll* (1957), which was in part a variation on one of the themes of *Cat on a Hot Tin Roof*, that of the seductive childish wife.

The following year saw the première of Williams's *Orpheus Descending*, a revised version of his 1940 play *Battle of Angels*. The reviews were lukewarm and Williams began to worry about becoming a failure. At this anxious. time he had news of his father's death. Latterly Williams had begun to see his father in a kindlier light, perhaps because he had freed himself of his mother's suffocating influence. The unexpected pain of his death seems to have precipitated a personal crisis; ever a hypochondriac and given to bouts of depression, Williams now embarked on a period of intensive psychotherapy (1957–8). It was already a very fashionable thing to do, but Williams, like a true professional, had another reason for taking this course of action. He hoped that psychoanalysis would free him of his obsession with madness and death and so broaden his dramatic range.

This was not to be, however, and his first play following his psychoanalysis, *Suddenly Last Summer*, returned yet again to the tragedy of his sister and to his relationship with his mother. In the play Mrs Venable tries to have her niece lobotomised in order to silence her and so protect the reputation of her homosexual son. If the dreadful Mrs Venable is Williams's mother, and her niece Catherine the victimised Rose, it would seem that her son Sebastian represents the darker side of Williams, the rich cruising homosexual. For the first time perhaps, Williams portrays himself not as a victim, an outsider rejected by society, but as a rapacious exploiter, a heartless lover of one-night stands who shrinks from emotional commitment. (Though Williams had had a stable relationship with his lover Frank Merlo since 1948, he utterly rejected any idea of fidelity, causing Frank much pain over the years.) *Suddenly Last Summer* was staged on Broadway in 1958, and to Williams's surprise proved a success, and not entirely just a *succès de scandale*.

The following year, 1959, brought his next play, *Sweet Bird of Youth*, yet another autobiographical soul-searching in disguise. Speaking through its heroine, an ageing film actress, Williams confesses his own sins of drunkenness, drug-taking and sexual exploitation. But shocking frankness alone does not make for a good play, and *Sweet Bird of Youth*, though a box office success thanks to its Gothic horrors (which include castration) was an artistic failure. The film industry, however, continued to court Williams, the film moguls being enthusiastically supportive of a formula that had proved successful in the past. Williams became wealthier still on the film rights of *Suddenly Last Summer* and *Sweet Bird of Youth*. He was rich, he was famous but he was starting to have doubts about the quality of his work.

Though troubled, he continued with his writing. As well as revising *Period of Adjustment*, an earlier 1958 play, he began writing *The Night of the Iguana*, while growing more and more dependent on drugs to silence his self-doubts. He became paranoid and turned against his best friends, including his agent, Audrey Wood, and his lover Frank Merlo. After several revisions *The Night of the Iguana* was finally presented in New York in December 1961, and in spite of the author's fears, was a success. It is an interesting play for the student of Williams's work, significantly different from most of his earlier plays in that it is set in Mexico, and not in the American South. Unusually, it ends on a note of hope for regeneration and it is quite free of the sensationalist horrors of so much of his work.

A few months later Williams went to Europe once more to start work on his next play. *The Milk Train Doesn't Stop Here Any More* was first staged in July 1962 at the Spoleto Festival in Italy, with only moderate success. It was at this time that news of a more deeply distressing kind came: Frank Merlo, with whom Williams had parted on bad terms, was ill with cancer. He was to die later, in September 1963. This was a painful period for Williams, racked with self-reproach over his treatment of his gentle, loyal companion. Inevitably he turned to drugs for comfort. Wealthy and famous, he found it easy to get all the fashionable anti-depressants and tranquillisers (all of them addictive) that he wanted. He drank steadily as well, living through what he later called his 'Stoned Age'. During this terrible time he still managed to write two one-act plays, staged jointly in January 1966 as *Slapstick Tragedy*. The reviews were bad, however, and the double bill closed after only seven performances.

During 1966 his drug intake increased alarmingly due to the criminal negligence – or greed – of his medical adviser. Confused and numbed by drugs, he still went on with his work (his prodigious creative energy seems to have been almost an instinct for self-preservation: as long as he went on writing, he stayed alive). His next play, *Kingdom of Earth* (renamed *The Seven Descents of Myrtle*) was staged in 1968, and flopped. Williams was so confused by drugs by this time that the play's failure passed by him unnoticed. His physical condition was so bad that his friends finally contacted his brother Dakin. He arrived to find Williams almost blind and hardly able to speak or walk. Dakin, a Roman Catholic convert, persuaded his befuddled brother to enter the Roman Catholic Church. Though the newspapers, always eager for newsworthy items about Williams, made much of his conversion, it is doubtful whether he ever regarded his action as significant, except perhaps as a belated tribute to Frank Merlo, who was himself a devout Catholic.

His next play, *In the Bar of a Tokyo Hotel*, opened in May 1969 and closed again. Its failure hardly touched the comatose writer, who remained equally indifferent to an honorary degree from his alma mater, the University of Missouri, and to an award from the National Institute of Arts and Letters. He was barely aware of his surroundings, yet insisted on moving from place to place, going as far as Japan. His paranoia grew worse and his friends found him impossible to deal with. Following an accident with a pot of scalding hot coffee his brother finally persuaded him to enter a hospital in St Louis. The treatment was drastic: all drugs were withdrawn at once, and he suffered several epileptic fits and two heart attacks. The prevailing ignorance about withdrawal symptoms seems strange to us now, but apparently no-one had anticipated such a violent reaction, and once it had taken place, Williams was not expected to survive. But survive he did and he repaid his brother by disinheriting him completely. His terror of being confined in a mental hospital is understandable in the light of Rose's tragedy, and this alone accounts for his implacable rejection of his brother.

For the rest of his life he continued to work with his usual manic energy but the results of his diligence were rarely satisfactory to him or popular with his critics. As his old friends died he took up with a new crowd in Key West, many of them hangers-on, greedy for money or vicarious fame. He went back to drugs too; his paranoia returned, and he broke off publicly with Audrey Wood at the opening of his new play *Out Cry* (Chicago, 1972), another failure. His next play, *Confessional* (retitled *Small Craft Warnings*), appeared on Broadway in 1973, as did *Out Cry*, no more successful in New York than it had been in Chicago. As if to underline the decline of his dramatic skills, there were already revivals of his earlier, better plays all over the United States.

Still he went on writing. *The Red Devil Battery Sign* opened in 1975 in Boston, and was a flop. Williams now turned to writing his *Memoirs*, which he had planned as an impressionist record but which in reality appeared chaotic and incomprehensible. A novel came next, *Moise and the World of Reason*, which failed disastrously. This was to be the pattern of his life from now on: revising old plays, starting on new ones and abandoning them. He felt a desperate need to write, perhaps to keep his private demons at bay or to exorcise them. He wrote poetry, much of it on openly homosexual themes, and another play, *Vieux Carré*, yet another failure. He was drinking and taking drugs as much as ever, and his behaviour was erratic and often abusive. In 1980 his mother died, but by then his condition was such that it is hard to tell what effect her death had on him.

There were some bright days ahead still: his play *A House Not Meant to Stand* (1982) was a reasonable success. By and large, however, Williams was a sad and lonely man, suffering from depression. After another spell in hospital he travelled alone to Taormina in Sicily, a place full of old memories of Frank. However he remained there for only a few days, returning to New York to stay at the Elysée Hotel. (There is dramatic irony in the hotel's name that Williams himself would have appreciated: the setting of his own *A Streetcar Named Desire* is the similarly titled Elysian Fields.) On 24 February 1983 he went to bed as usual with a bottle of wine and a trayful of drugs. In the morning he was found dead in bed; the overcap of one of his barbiturates had become lodged in his throat and, unable to call for help, he had died alone.

A note on the text

First begun in 1945, *A Streetcar Named Desire* went through several metamorphoses before Williams settled on its final form. He worked on the first version, entitled *The Moth*, early in 1945, and returned to it a little later, renaming the second version *Blanche's Chair in the Moon*. By the summer of 1945 the play was renamed yet again, *The Poker Night*. With the changes in the title came other adjustments as well. Originally the family at the centre was Italian, then the brother-in-law became Irish and the two sisters turned into Southern belles. Later again the chief male character became a Polish-American. The changes make it clear that Williams regarded class clash as a crucial element in the play.

It was first published in book form in the United States by New Directions, New York, in 1947, and reissued with an introduction by the author by New American Library, New York, in 1951. An acting edition was brought out by the Dramatists' Play Service, New York, in 1953.

In the UK, *A Streetcar Named Desire* was first published in 1949 by John Lehmann, London, and in 1956 it was reissued by Secker & Warburg, London, in a collection entitled *Four Plays*. A paperback edition published by Penguin Books, Harmondsworth, in their Penguin Plays contains also *Sweet Bird of Youth* and *The Glass Menagerie*. It has now been incorporated into the Penguin Twentieth Century Classics series.

In 1984 Methuen brought out the Methuen Student Edition of the play, with notes by Patricia Hern, and with stills from the film version. The 1994 reprint of this edition was used in the preparation of these Notes.

The stage history of *A Streetcar Named Desire* is also of interest. It was first staged in the United States under the direction of Elia Kazan in November 1947 in Boston, and in December of the same year in New York, with Jessica Tandy and Marlon Brando in the two leading parts. The part of Blanche was later taken, in turn, by Uta Hagen and Tallulah Bankhead, while Anthony Quinn took Brando's place for a short time. The British première was in 1949 at the Aldwych Theatre in London, with Laurence Olivier directing. Vivien Leigh played Blanche and Bonnar Colleano Stanley. In 1951 a film version of the play was made, with Kazan directing, and Leigh and Brando playing the leading parts.

Part 2

Summaries
of A STREETCAR
NAMED DESIRE

A general summary

The play is set in a working-class area of New Orleans in a street called Elysian Fields. Stanley Kowalski and his wife Stella live in a rented apartment in a run-down house owned by Eunice and her husband Steve. An incongruously dainty woman arrives carrying a suitcase. She is Stella's older sister, Blanche DuBois, arriving on a visit. She is dismayed to find herself in such surroundings, but accepts the landlady's invitation to wait for her sister. When Stella returns, the sisters' meeting is affectionate yet strained.

On his return home Stanley accepts Blanche's presence amiably enough, but tensions develop quickly. We hear that Blanche had been married but that her husband is now dead. It becomes clear that she has somehow lost the family property, Belle Reve, and Stanley suspects her of dishonesty.

After a poker party, during which the sisters had been absent on a visit to the theatre, Stanley, who is now drunk, shows his jealousy of Blanche and his resentment at her interest in one of his poker-playing friends, the gentle, shy Mitch. A violent scene follows and Stanley hits Stella who is pregnant. The hysterical Blanche removes her sister upstairs to Eunice's apartment, but is shocked to discover later that Stella has returned to her husband and gone to bed with him.

The next day Stella makes it clear to Blanche that in spite of her husband's brutality she has no intention of leaving him. Stanley overhears Blanche's hostile comments on himself, and his resentment grows. He takes the trouble to check on Blanche's past and discovers that she more or less had to leave her home town, Laurel, because of her promiscuity. He hints at his knowledge to her, and she is obviously terrified. She tries to explain to her sister the motives for her past behaviour and her terror of growing old alone, but is unable to speak of her past honestly. She confesses, though, that she hopes to marry Mitch.

Mitch and Blanche go out for an evening together, but the occasion is a disaster, in spite of (or perhaps because of) Blanche's hectic girlish gaiety. They return to the empty apartment, and sit in the dark, talking more easily in a friendly fashion. Blanche tells Mitch of her disastrous marriage and we learn from her hints that her husband turned out to be homosexual, and that he shot himself after she had discovered him in bed with another man. Mitch comforts her, and they come to an understanding that they will get married.

There is to be a special birthday dinner for Blanche to which Mitch has been invited. However, Stanley now has the full details of Blanche's scandalous past, and has told Mitch about it. Mitch never turns up for the dinner. After a ghastly silent meal Stanley presents Blanche with a birthday gift – a bus ticket to Laurel, with her seat booked. Stella reproaches her husband for his cruelty, but their quarrel is interrupted when her childbirth contractions begin and Stanley takes her to the hospital.

Left alone in the apartment, Blanche has a visit from Mitch. He has been drinking, and tells her brutally that he knows all about her past and will no longer listen to any of her lies. Blanche tries to explain the reasons for her behaviour in the past, but her pathetic plea is dismissed as yet more lies. To show her his contempt for her, he tries to rape her, but runs off when she threatens to raise the alarm.

Blanche is once more alone in the apartment. Befuddled by drink and lost in her delusions and fantasies, she dresses up dazedly in a ball gown and puts on a cheap tiara, while trying to pack her suitcase. Stanley returns, having been sent home to rest as the baby is not due for some hours. He has been drinking and now he mocks Blanche's confused fabrications about a rich admirer and a cruise. Brutally, he tells her what he thinks of her. His antagonism, which always had a sexual tinge in it, is transformed into sexual violence, and he carries the terrified, fainting Blanche to the bed to rape her.

A few weeks later we witness the final scene of the tragedy. Stella, unwilling to believe her sister's story as the truth, has connived with her husband to have the unstable Blanche certified insane. She is now packing Blanche's things while her sister is having yet another bath, preparing, as she believes, to depart with her rich admirer.

In the midst of these feverish preparations Stanley and his friends are playing another game of poker, though Stanley alone seems calm enough to concentrate on the game. A doctor arrives with the matron of a mental institution, and there is a painful scene when Blanche, suddenly aware of the threat to her, tries to escape. The doctor's gentleness calms her down and she leaves on his arm with the grim matron following. Stanley seems unmoved but his friends are aghast, and Stella sobs uncontrollably, overcome by grief and remorse. Her husband's voluptuous caresses soothe her into calmness; life will go on as before, perhaps.

Detailed summaries

Scene 1

The play opens outside a shabby house in a poor district of New Orleans. Eunice, the owner of the building, is sitting on the steps with a black neighbour. Stanley Kowalski enters with his friend Mitch on his way to a bowling alley, and his wife Stella follows them to watch the game. Blanche DuBois enters, a delicate figure who is out of place in these surroundings. She is horrified to find that this is the house she is looking for, and explains that she has come to visit her sister, Mrs Kowalski. Eunice lets her into the apartment and is dismissed by Blanche to fetch Stella.

Alone, Blanche finds a bottle of whisky and helps herself to a drink. She is evidently in an overwrought, nervous state. Her sister returns, and though they embrace affectionately, the emotional meeting does not disguise a latent unease. When Blanche is openly critical of the shabby apartment, Stella tries to warn her that life is different in New Orleans, and that her husband, the son of a Polish immigrant, is not like the gentlemen admirers of the sisters' girlhood. Plainly, she is quite happy in her new life, and deeply in love with her husband. As the sisters talk uneasily, Blanche reveals that she had to sell Belle Reve, the family estate, to pay for the doctors' bills and funerals of their relations. Stanley returns with Mitch and Eunice's husband, Steve. Stanley accepts the news of Blanche's visit easily enough, but Blanche is taken aback by his coarse manner. She tells him that she had been married but that her husband died young.

NOTES AND GLOSSARY:

Epigraph: an author's choice of the quotation introducing his work is invariably significant, and can be regarded as a clue to what he sees as the main theme of his work. For this play Williams chose a stanza from 'The Broken Tower' by Hart Crane (1899–1932), an American poet hardly read nowadays. In the course of his short life (he committed suicide by jumping off the ship he was travelling on) he published two books of verse, *White Buildings* and *The Bridge*, both marked by a complex and highly individual rhetoric. 'The Broken Tower', one of the last poems he wrote, expresses the poet's sense of isolation (Crane was a homosexual), of his doomed search for an elusive happiness. The parallel with Blanche's desperate snatchings at love needs hardly be stressed

Elysian Fields: in classical mythology this is the place to which those favoured by the gods go after death to enjoy a pleasant after-life. The irony of such a name being given to a run-down street is obvious, but there is an additional significance for the play in it: as the name of the dwelling-place of the dead Elysian Fields may be a pointer to the living death that awaits Blanche

L & N tracks: the tracks of the Louisiana and Nashville Railroad

section: (*US*) district

it has a raffish charm: Williams's affection for New Orleans, where he lived, off and on, over a period of years, was rooted in its beauty as much as in its slightly shady character. Given that he was a homosexual at a time when homosexual practices were still illegal, it is not hard to understand why Williams felt at home in the unconventional, easy-going life of the 'Vieux Carré', the old part of New Orleans favoured by painters, writers and jazz musicians

white frame: the houses have wooden frames filled with stucco or plaster and painted white

tender blue: you should read the stage directions with care: the descriptions, matter-of-fact to begin with, soon start to use the language of poetry ('a peculiarly tender blue'). There are visual images, an emphasis on colour, and a vivid evocation of sounds and smells

Negro entertainers: black musicians playing and singing the blues were largely responsible for creating the atmosphere characteristic of New Orleans. (The word 'Negro' – now no longer acceptable – was not used in an abusive sense then)

the infatuated fluency of brown fingers: a phrase capturing a black pianist's speed, skill and total absorption

"Blue Piano": the blues encapsulate the spirit of New Orleans

coloured: used in the US for 'black'

St. Barnabas: the black woman may be thinking of St Bernard, the rescuer of travellers in the Alps, after whom St Bernard's dogs are named

the Four Deuces: the name of a night-club or bar

Red hot!: the vendor's description of the spicy food he is selling

clip joint: a night-club where the customers are overcharged and cheated (clipped like sheep)

a Blue Moon cocktail: a drink which will knock the customer out

you won't go out on your own feet!: you will be carried out dead drunk

bowling jacket: brightly coloured jacket for tenpin bowling

a red-stained package: the blood-stained parcel of meat introduces a warning note of violence

even money ... odds: betting terms; even money is a bet of equal sums on both possible outcomes, while odds is a bet which will win more than the amount wagered

Naw!: a vulgar form of No!

holler: (*US*) shout

a poor boy's sandwich: a sandwich made of a French loaf split lengthwise, buttered and filled with slices of meat

valise: (*US*) suitcase

something ... *that suggests a moth*: a significant phrase describing Blanche's fragile beauty, but hinting at its passing, symbolised by the short life of a moth. We may recall here that the play's first title was *The Moth*

a streetcar named Desire: Williams remembered the curious name and destination of a streetcar (tramcar) from his New Orleans days. The symbolism would have appealed to his sense of the macabre as much as to his ironic humour

blocks: a block is the part of a street between two intersecting streets

You don't have to look no further: this is the place you are looking for

That's the party: that's the person

I got the up: I have the upper floor

Por nada: (*Spanish*) not at all

taught school: (*US*) were a teacher

Belle Reve: the name of the plantation, like the sisters' family name, DuBois, indicates that the family was of French, probably Huguenot (French Protestant) origin. The name probably means 'Beautiful dream', though, if correctly written in French, it would be Beau Rêve

A great big place with white columns: description of a typical Southern mansion built in Colonial style. The wealth of the South was founded on cotton and tobacco, and the large mansions were mostly owned by planters who employed slave labour. Mississippi, like Louisiana, of which New Orleans is the chief port, was one of the Confederate Southern states which broke off from the Union in 1861 in order to maintain the slavery system. In the Civil War that followed (1861–5) the Confederacy was the loser

awful hard to keep up: very expensive to run

just about to drop: very tired

set down: (*US*) sit down

make myself scarce: leave

hustle her up: make her hurry back

I've got to keep hold of myself!: Blanche makes excuses for her drinking even to herself, pretending that she is only drinking to steady her nerves *a spasmodic embrace*: the sisters embrace with an almost hysterical intensity to cover their unease

over-light: ceiling light

I spy, I spy!: phrase from a children's game. The note of artificial gaiety betrays Blanche's nervous discomfort

Edgar Allan Poe: American poet of the macabre (1809–49), who also wrote a number of Gothic horror tales. Blanche is hardly complimentary about the Kowalskis' apartment

the ghoul-haunted woodland of Weir: a quotation from Poe's poem 'Ulalumé', reminding us that Blanche was formerly an English teacher

tamping: pressing down

watch around the hips a little: be careful you don't put on weight round the hips. The comment shows that Blanche is unaware of her sister's pregnancy

I said stand up: we realise now that Blanche, being several years older, is used to bossing her sister

feather bob: hair cut short to frame the face softly

put the stopper on: put the cork back into the bottle, stop drinking

haven't slipped one particle: haven't deteriorated even the tiniest bit

that gives much: that is too soft

Stanley is Polish: Stella means that Stanley is not very refined and the lack of privacy will not bother him

Polacks: contemptuous American nickname for people of Polish origin

blinded by all the brass: dazzled by his uniform and all the decorations

looked out for yourself: took care of your own interests

The music of the "blue piano" . . .: the sound of blues played on the piano recurs in the play at moments of dramatic significance. Williams uses music throughout not just to create a mood, but to stress directly the significance of what is happening on the stage

So big with it: so swollen by disease

sometimes it rattles: a dying person sometimes makes a rattling sound in the throat

the Grim Reaper: the personification of death, often represented as a skeleton holding a scythe to cut people down like grass

left a cent of insurance: had paid for any insurance (to cover the cost of their last illness and funeral)

In bed: the coarse sexual allusion is particularly jarring after the talk of death. It also hints at Blanche's jealousy of her sister

is Mass out yet: a base joke depending on an exaggerated pronuncia-
tion of 'Mass' to make it sound like 'my ass'
Break it up: stop making that noise
Jax beer: beer from Jacksonville, Florida
the gaudy seed-bearer: the flashily dressed, potent male
the little woman: a patronisingly jocular way of referring to one's wife
Laurel: town in Mississippi
Not in my territory: not in the area I cover as a travelling salesman
Liquor goes fast in hot weather: Stanley's remark is clearly ironic. For
all his coarseness he is a shrewd judge of people
depletion: act of emptying
Have a shot?: would you like some whisky?
Some people rarely touch it . . . often: Stanley's shrewdness shows itself
again: people who claim that they hardly ever drink
are quite often heavy drinkers
shack up: stay with us
Haven't fallen in: one of Stanley's jokes: you haven't fallen into the
lavatory bowl, have you?
The music of the polka: this is the second musical motif, representing
Blanche's brief marriage. The jolly dance tune is in
stark contrast to the tragedy it recalls

Scene II

The following evening the sisters are planning to go out together so
as to keep out of the way of Stanley's poker party. While Blanche is
having a bath, Stanley questions his wife about the loss of Belle Reve. He
obviously suspects Blanche of having swindled her sister out of her share
of the profits of the sale which he claims as his share too. He rummages in
Blanche's trunk, displaying her cheap finery as proof of her ill-gotten
wealth. (Stanley misinterprets her fake jewellery for the real thing.) Stella
walks away in anger just as Blanche emerges from the bathroom in a
cheerful, flirtatious mood to which Stanley reacts with sullen resentment.
He demands to see the papers relating to the sale of the estate, and in the
ensuing scuffle he seizes a bundle of old love letters from Blanche's dead
husband. She is distressed but eventually produces the legal documents of
the sale. Apologising indirectly for his behaviour, Stanley explains that
financial affairs of the family matter to him more now that his wife is
expecting a baby. In an atmosphere of reconciliation the sisters leave for
their evening out.

NOTES AND GLOSSARY:
the perpetual "blue piano": the piano music is a constant reminder of the
sensuous presence of New Orleans

monkey doings: silly nonsense (meaning the sisters' preparations for their evening out)

with lordly composure: Stanley accepts his wife's devotion as his due

not going to no Galatoire's: the ungrammatical use of a double negative stresses Stanley's lack of education

a cold plate: a plate of cold meat and salad

dandy: delightful (used ironically)

tub: (*US*) bath

gloss things over: omit the mention of anything disagreeable

So that's the deal: so that's the arrangement

I saw how she was: Stanley implies that Blanche was drunk, not ill

a gander: a quick look

bill of sale: formal document confirming the sale of a property

Napoleonic code: the 'Code Napoléon', a code of laws prepared in 1800–1804 under the direction of Napoleon I after he became Emperor of France. The code forms the basis of modern French law. One of the points of the system was a husband's right to all his wife's property upon marriage. Louisiana had been a French colony but it was purchased by the United States in 1803 so that there never had been a time when the Code Napoléon was in operation there. Nevertheless Stanley is obsessed by the code, which he seems to regard as something of a magic formula

A solid-gold dress: a dress made of woven gold thread would certainly have been an expensive item, but it was probably made of gold lamé or some such material

appraise it: estimate the value of it

daybed: sofa which can be converted into a bed at night

costume jewellery: cheap imitation jewellery

rhinestone tiara: circular hair ornament decorated with imitation diamonds

You're damn tootin': you are damned right

robe: (*US*) dressing-gown

drapes: (*US*) curtains

a drag on your cig: a puff of your cigarette

fishing for a compliment: saying something in order to receive a compliment

a doll: (*US*) a woman

took in: taken in, deceived

Lay ... her cards on the table: speak plainly and truthfully. Stanley imbues the word 'lay' with sexual innuendo

wishy-washy: colourless, uninteresting

re-bop: (*US slang*) nonsensical chatter

I'm through dressing: I have finished dressing

drug-store: in the US much more than a chemist's shop, it sells
                         drinks, ice cream and so on

lemon-coke: Coca-Cola with lemonade

double-talk: words with a hidden meaning

atomizer: perfume spray

The first anniversary gift ... papers!: Blanche is referring to the first
                         wedding anniversary which is traditionally known as
                         the paper anniversary

Don't pull that stuff!: stop pretending!

made loans on the place: lent money with the property as security

epic fornications: sexual misbehaviour on a grand scale

The "blue piano" sounds louder: the music stresses the importance of
                         Stanley's announcement

thrashed it out: talked it over thoroughly

TAMALE: crisp cornmeal biscuits with a spicy meat filling

Red hots!:   the tamale vendor's cry, but to Blanche it is perhaps a
                         reminder of sexual passion and of the past she is
                         trying to hide

The blind are – leading the blind!: a proverb (see the Bible, Matthew
                         14:15) which means that those unqualified to lead are
                         leading others equally unqualified. The implication is
                         that disaster is imminent, and this is underlined here
                         by Blanche's desperate laughter

the "blue piano" and the hot trumpet: the blues music played on the
                         piano is counterpointed here by a jazz trumpet

---

Scene III

It is 2.30 in the morning and Stanley, Mitch, Steve and Pablo are still
playing poker when Stella and Blanche return. Mitch is obviously interested in Blanche, and, equally obviously, she is aware of his attention.
Stanley is now quite drunk and his temper gets worse. The sound of the
sisters' conversation from the next room annoys him and when Blanche
switches on the radio to dance to the music Stanley in a rage throws it out
of the window. In the ensuing quarrel he hits Stella and the outraged
Blanche takes her upstairs to Eunice's apartment. The men gather round
Stanley to calm him down and sober him up. He calls for Stella until she
appears and a passionate reconciliation scene follows. Blanche is appalled
to find that Stella has gone back to her husband, but Mitch comforts her.

NOTES AND GLOSSARY:

The Poker Night: this was the third title of the play, and might almost
                         be the title of one of Van Gogh's paintings

a picture of Van Gogh's: Vincent Van Gogh (1853–90), Dutch painter of the Post-Impressionist school, noted for his masterly use of colour and light. As well as for sun-drenched Provençal landscapes he is known for his lamplit interiors which'are vivid and often rather grotesque

the raw colours of childhood's spectrum: clear primary colours such as children use. (Notice the repeated use of colours in this description of the stage setting: we can almost see the men's shirts glowing in the dimly lit room and the bright pink of the watermelon on the table)

portières: curtains across the door to provide privacy as well as fresh air

absorbed: intensely concentrated

wild: a card with a value to be decided by the players

One-eyed jacks: knaves of spades and hearts in a pack of cards, seen in profile on the card and therefore with one eye showing only

I'm out: I'm not playing

a shot: a drink of neat whisky

the Chinaman's: the Chinese takeaway

chop suey: a westernised form of Chinese food

Ante up!:   raise the amount of money we are playing for!

Openers?:   who is going to make the opening bid?

chips: money staked by the players (sometimes tokens – known as chips – are used instead of money)

lurches up: gets to his feet unsteadily

oughta . . . gotta: colloquial pronunciation of ought to, got to

Spade flush: a hand consisting entirely of spades

sugar-tit: a baby's teat flavoured with sugar

lay off: stop teasing me

Seven card stud: variety of poker in which the aim is to collect the best hand possible, each player concealing some of his cards and making a guess at the hands of the other players. The word 'stud' means also a male horse kept for breeding purposes, and may be taken here to be a hint at Stanley's sexuality

ole nigger: old black man (an insulting term)

lickety split: running fast

puts on the brakes: stops suddenly

gits *that* hongry: get so hungry that I lose all interest in sex

frazzled: tired out

done in: exhausted

took in a show: went to a theatre

Please don't get up: courtesy to women was part of the social code of the South and Blanche assumes that the men will stand up as she comes in

quit: stop

kibitz: watch the game (and offer unwanted advice to the players)

call it quits: decide to stop playing

a wolf: a man who pursues women for sexual conquest

precision bench: part of a factory where more delicate work is carried out

plant: (*US*) factory

drive: forceful character

Oh, am I!: the implication is that Blanche is quite aware that she can be seen from the other room

beefy: heavily built

hens: a derogatory name for women, implying that they are silly and noisy like hens

cut out: stop

Xavier Cugat: popular American band-leader, associated with Latin-American dance music

the "head": the lavatory

got ants: short for 'got ants in his pants', got jumpy

spitballs: small pieces of paper chewed up and rolled into balls

quarters: 25 cent coins

Spit in the Ocean: a kind of poker game

The Little Boys' Room: a coy euphemism for a lavatory

wrapper: dressing-gown

Luckies: Lucky Strikes, a brand of cigarettes

"And if God choose ... after – death!": a quotation from *Sonnets from the Portuguese*, 43, by Elizabeth Barrett Browning (1806–61), wife of the poet Robert Browning, and a distinguished poet in her own right

My tongue is a little – thick: Blanche is drunk and cannot pronounce the word 'superficial'

The show let out: the play finished

Deal me out: start playing without me

Huguenots: French Calvinists (Protestants, followers of Jean Calvin (1509–64). They survived both the Massacre of St Bartholomew (24 August 1572), when some 50,000 of them were murdered, and the religious wars that followed, but were finally driven out by religious intolerance in the seventeenth century. They eventually settled in the Low Countries, in England, South Africa and the American Colonies)

she's somewhat older than I: Blanche's vanity makes her lie; Stella is in fact several years younger

Bourbon: the main street in the French Quarter of New Orleans

run down: tired

teach school: (*US*) be a teacher

Grade school or high school: (*US*) primary or secondary school (though the divisions do not exactly correspond to the British educational system)

instructor: teacher

bobby-soxers: teenage girls

drug-store Romeos: adolescent boys who meet their girlfriends in the local drug-store

Hawthorne: Nathaniel Hawthorne (1804–64), American novelist, author of *The Scarlet Letter* and *The House with Seven Gables*

Whitman: Walt Whitman (1819–92), American poet, whose *Leaves of Grass*, written in free verse, is an influential work of passion and originality

Poe: see notes on Scene I above

"Wien, Wien, nur du allein": 'Vienna, Vienna, you alone', the title of a popular Viennese waltz

pinioned: held down with his arms at his sides

blew your top: lost your temper completely

sons of bitches: common US term of abuse

polka dot drawers: spotted underpants

baby doll: term of endearment

Dissonant brass and piano sounds ... a brief interval: once again the music continues the action, the dissonant chords repeating the quarrel, and the blue piano concluding the scene with a note of sadness and loss

Quit that howling: stop bellowing

you'll git th' law on you: the police will come for you

beat on a woman: hit a woman

you whelp of a Polack: you contemptible Polish puppy

The low-tone clarinet moans: the music is now charged with sexual passion

catches her breath as if struck: Blanche realises that Stella is back with her husband, making love. She feels a sense of shocked betrayal, even fear

All quiet on the Potomac: a phrase originating from the American Civil War, and attributed to General George McClellan (1826–85) who forced the Southern forces back over the river Potomac in 1862

Naw: no

Set down:	sit down. (Through his use of ungrammatical speech forms we are made aware that Mitch is Blanche's inferior socially)

Scene IV

Early the following morning Blanche enters the Kowalskis' bedroom in great agitation. Stanley is already gone and Stella is still in bed, lazy and contented after the night's love-making. She tries to make Blanche understand the nature of her passionate relationship with Stanley but Blanche refuses to listen. She is convinced that her sister must be rescued from her brutal husband and she hopes that a rich old admirer of hers will finance their new life together. Her tirade against Stanley is overheard by him but when he makes his presence known, Stella shows by the warmth of her embrace that her love and loyalty lie with her husband.

NOTES AND GLOSSARY:

like a choral chant: the ritual cries of the street vendors blend to resemble a church choir

a book of coloured comics: a small detail that reminds us that Stella now belongs to a world where comics, not books, are read

narcotized tranquillity: drug-induced peace

sloppy: messy, untidy

get the car greased: have lubricating oil put on the axles of the car

I'm glad you didn't: Blanche would have found her sister in bed with Stanley

a powder-keg: a potentially explosive situation

matter of fact: sensible, practical

fix: awkward situation

movies: (*US*) films

I guess: (*US*) I suppose

wore his pin: wore the ornamental pin of his fraternity (men's college society) to show that she was his girlfriend

Miami: seaside city in Florida, still a holiday resort today

ran into: met by chance

Cadillac convertible: expensive car with a folding roof

must have been a block long!: American cars were, and still are to some extent, extremely long, the longer the more expensive and calculated to impress

Texas ... gold in his pockets: Texas oil-wells are earning him a lot of money

My, my: ironic expression of admiration and wonder

Western Union: one of the main telephone companies in the United States

in coin of the realm: in coins (now used mostly facetiously)
to smooth things over: to make the atmosphere pleasant again after the quarrel
take to the streets: become a prostitute
bromo: tranquillising drug, especially for curing a headache
let things go: stop worrying
one of those mysterious electric things: love at first sight
rattle-trap: noisy, rickety
bangs: the verb means 'make a noise' but it is also a slang term for sexual intercourse (which links with the destination of the streetcar, 'Desire')
when the devil is in you: when you feel reckless
seersucker pants: trousers made of a puckered cotton fabric
bestial: Blanche is very aware of Stanley's sexuality
Bearing the raw meat home: the audience will recall Stanley's first appearance with the blood-stained parcel
swilling: drinking greedily and untidily
gnawing: chewing meat off the bone
hulking: moving clumsily
Hiyuh: Hi, you (a colloquial greeting)
Them darn mechanics: those damned mechanics
don't know their can ... base: don't know anything; ('can' can mean a car battery, but also, the buttocks; 'third base' is a term from baseball)
the music of the "blue piano" and trumpet and drums: a note of triumph and exultation

---

Scene V

Eunice and Steve are having a row, with Stanley and Stella as amused bystanders. Stanley asks Blanche about her acquaintance with a man called Shaw, who claims to have seen her in a disreputable hotel in Laurel, the Flamingo. Blanche tries to turn his questions aside lightly but it is obvious that she is frightened. Stanley leaves and Blanche tries to explain to her sister, as obliquely as she can, that there are incidents in her past which reflect badly on her and that she had been forced to behave as she had done by her desperate need to attract a man. She is frightened of growing old and losing her looks and confesses to Stella that she very much hopes to marry Mitch. Later, waiting for Mitch, Blanche flirts with a young man who calls to collect the subscription for a newspaper. She kisses him and sends him off. She is now ready to greet Mitch gaily.

NOTES AND GLOSSARY:
on the wing: moving constantly

Forewarned is forearmed: a proverb meaning that if one has advance warning of an approaching danger, one can prepare oneself for it

Gulf: Gulf of Mexico

ain't pulling the wool over my eyes: aren't deceiving me

stay down: stay downstairs in the bar of the Four Deuces, drinking

going up: going upstairs to the prostitutes' bedrooms

vice squad: section of the police which deals with prostitution and gambling

Don't throw that at me!: Eunice is about to throw some kitchen utensil at Steve

daemonic: passionately angry, as if possessed by demons

Some of your sister's friends: an ironic reference to the lies in Blanche's letter

bowling shirt: brightly coloured shirt worn for bowling

registers: shows her awareness of

That hunk!: that fat lump! (a scornful reference to his wife's size)

You won't pick up ... before: Stanley's reply prepares the way for his later innuendos about Blanche's past

count on: rely on (Stanley's answer uses the verb in its literal meaning)

Astrological sign: according to astrology, a pseudo-science much in fashion today, a person's character is influenced by the date of his or her birth. A calendar year is divided into twelve signs of the Zodiac, constellations of stars on an imaginary belt in the heavens. The Zodiacal sign appropriate for those born in that particular part of the year will exercise a distinctive influence on their character and ultimately their fate

Aries: the Zodiacal sign of the Ram. Traditionally the ram is often associated with base sexuality

banging: see the notes on Scene IV for the double meaning of this word

is under the impression: Stanley is careful not to be too definite about what he had heard from Shaw

I figure: (*US*) I suppose

some other party: some other person

cooing: murmuring softly and lovingly

Don't I rate one kiss?: don't I deserve a kiss?

slip through my fingers: slip out of my control, be lost through negligence

the colours of butterfly wings: we may remember here Williams's description of Blanche on her first appearance in

Scene I (*'There is something about her ... that suggests a moth'*.)

put a – paper lantern over the light: we remember here Blanche putting a paper lantern over a light bulb in Scene III, an action symbolising her constant struggle to hide the ugliness of reality. Her hesitant speech here, when she is trying to explain herself to Stella, is yet another attempt to hide the reality of her promiscuous past

awf'ly: awfully. (A characteristic of Southern speech is a soft drawl, slurring the words)

turn the trick: be successful

I'm fading now: I am losing my beauty now

you want a shot in it: you want some whisky in it

hang around: stay on when no longer wanted

gives a piercing cry: it may be that the stain on her white skirt reminds Blanche of her husband's suicide

hasn't gotten a thing: has not had intimate relations with me

put out: make blatant use of her physical attractions

with a drink under his belt: having had a drink or two

Trumpet and drums: a joyous celebration of pleasure

The music from the Four Deuces ... blue: the mood changes as the play focuses on Blanche

cackling: laughing wildly

She says something indistinguishable: probably an indecent proposal

collecting for *The Evening Star*: collecting the money due from the paper's subscribers

a dime: 10 cents, the smallest US coin

Fifteen of seven: a quarter to seven

the "blue piano" is heard: the continuous music underlines the significance of this little scene. We are made to realise that however anxious Blanche may be to marry Mitch, she will risk her chance of a safe haven for a sexual adventure. We are reminded also of her reputed penchant for young boys

soda: fizzy soft drink

You make my mouth water: there is a sexual undercurrent in Blanche's words

the Arabian Nights: a famous collection of Eastern tales

I've got to be good ... off children: we are given a broad hint about the reasons for the abrupt end of Blanche's teaching career

Adios!: (*Spanish*) goodbye!

Rosenkavalier: (German for 'the Knight of the Rose') the title of an opera by Richard Strauss (1864–1949). The

Rosenkavalier is Octavian, a youth (the part is usually sung by a woman), and Blanche is mocking the sedate, middle-aged Mitch when calling him by that name

Bow to me first! Now present them: the mockery continues with Blanche's orders to Mitch

Merciiii!: an exaggerated pronunciation of *Merci* (French for 'thank you')

Scene VI

Blanche and Mitch return from their evening out in low spirits: in spite of Blanche's hectic efforts the evening has been a failure. Blanche flirts a little but when Mitch tries to kiss her she holds him off, insisting on her respectability. They sit in the dark and talk somewhat awkwardly. Mitch speaks of his mother who seems to be taking an interest in Blanche. As they speak more companionably Blanche is moved to talk of her young husband who committed suicide. It appears that he was homosexual and that he killed himself after Blanche caught him in bed with a man and then denounced him publicly. Mitch, moved by her story, embraces her and asks her to marry him. Blanche turns to him in gratitude, weeping.

NOTES AND GLOSSARY:

neurasthenic: suffering from weak nerves

Lake Pontchartrain: lake and park near New Orleans with a fairground

Mae West: (1893–1980) American film actress famous for her plump, seductive figure, her husky voice and the wit and sexual audacity of her jokes

shooting-galleries: places of entertainment where customers shoot at targets in the hope of a lucky hit and a prize

games of chance: games that depend on luck, usually the throw of dice, not on skill

hot tamale man: the vendor of spicy Mexican food whose voice had been heard in Scenes I and II

owl-car: an all-night tram

gotten: (*US*) got

rise to the occasion: act in the lively manner which was expected of her

ten points for trying: a joking reference to the system used by teachers for grading a child's schoolwork. A child will be awarded points for working hard even if he/she is not very bright. (Another reminder that Blanche had been a teacher)

no dice!: it's no use! the answer is no!

my fingers are all thumbs: I am clumsy

rooting: searching

outstayed my welcome: stayed longer than I was expected to

Eureka!: (Greek for 'I have found') exclamation used at the end of a successful search

Pleiades: in Greek mythology the seven daughters of Pleione and the giant Atlas. They were transformed into stars

going home from their little bridge party: Blanche imagines the Pleiades as seven suburban ladies returning from their regular bridge party

or she'll be lost!: or she will lose her good name and with it any hope of marrying

The lord and lady of the house: a mocking reference to the Kowalskis

a night-cap: a drink before bedtime

joie de vivre: (*French*) joy of living, sense of enjoyment

Bohemian: unconventional like an artist, free of the restrictions of social code

a little artists' cafe on the Left Bank in Paris: the (unrealistic) image of the University quarter of Paris, presented for instance in Giacomo Puccini's (1858–1924) opera *La Bohème* (1896)

Je suis la Dame aux Camellias!: (French for 'I'm the Lady of the Camellias') Marguerite Gautier, a high-class prostitute, who is the tragic heroine of Alexandre Dumas the Younger's (1824–95) novel of the same title

Vous êtes – Armand!: (*French*) you are Armand! Armand was Marguerite Gautier's lover whom she gave up at his father's request

Voulez-vous coucher . . . quel dommage!: (*French*) do you want to sleep with me tonight? You don't understand? Ah, what a pity!

alpaca: soft light woollen cloth

wash-coat: light washable cotton or linen jacket

Samson: ancient Hebrew hero of great strength who could only be defeated by the Philistines after Delilah betrayed him (see the Bible, Judges 16)

demureness: (false) modesty

unhand me: let go of me (a jocular phrase supposed to come from a popular melodrama)

step out of bounds: go beyond the permitted limits

I have – old-fashioned ideals: in this scene Blanche constantly uses phrases and expressions from a bygone age in an attempt to bring some romance to the situation and to give Mitch the impression that she is naïve and virtuous. Here she overtly states what she has been

	trying to imply. However, from what we know of her past, this is clearly not true
She rolls her eyes:	this gesture shows that Blanche is all too aware of the irony of her last statement
prevue:	performance before the official opening
Loew's State:	a cinema
the Two-forty-first:	the 241st Engineers, an army regiment
get along with him:	be on friendly terms with him

He stalks through the rooms ... isn't necessary: we cannot be certain that what Blanche says about Stanley is true but we do know that she herself is guilty of the same behaviour (see Scene III)

settled:	married
passes on:	euphemism for 'dies'
Deluded:	deceived

he wasn't the least bit effeminate looking: Blanche means that he was homosexual

in the quicksands: in great danger. (The quicksands are an area of treacherous loose, watery sand which can swallow up a person)

A locomotive is heard: the noise and glaring headlights of the train startle Blanche as she recalls the past. The locomotive also has a symbolic function and is representative of both her unpleasant past and her fate. Her extreme reaction to it shows the power of her memories over her mental state

Polka music sounds ... distance: this is the music of Blanche's tragic marriage, first heard in Scene I. It is now being played quietly in a minor key which makes its effect particularly sinister

the Varsouviana: the Warsaw polka

the Polka ... major key: the return to a major key represents the escalating force of the memory

the searchlight ... turned off again: Blanche never loved a man again

Sometimes – there's God – so quickly: as in Scenes II and III Blanche's words provide a dramatically effective ending

Scene VII

It is the late afternoon of Blanche's birthday, and Stella is laying the table for a special birthday supper while Blanche is having a bath. Stanley enters in a triumphant mood. He has been finding out about Blanche's life in Laurel and now he presents Stella with the facts. Blanche had been living in the Flamingo hotel and had been asked to leave even this doubtful establishment because of her promiscuity. She became so notorious that her room was declared out of bounds to the soldiers from the nearby army camp, and the townspeople thought she was insane. Her teaching career ended because she tried to seduce a pupil, a boy of seventeen, and in the end she was virtually forced to leave the town. Stanley warns Stella that Mitch is unlikely to come to the birthday supper, having been told all about Blanche's past. Stanley felt it his duty to warn him as an old friend. Blanche must leave, and to make sure that she does, he has bought her the bus ticket back to Laurel. At this point Blanche emerges at long last from the bathroom. She senses that something has happened and is frightened.

NOTES AND GLOSSARY:

Temperature 100 on the nose: the outside temperature is exactly 100° Fahrenheit

Set down: sit down

dope: inside information

rub her the wrong way: annoy her

the cat's out of the bag: the truth has come out

saccharine: sickly sentimental

contrapuntally: a musical term meaning as an accompaniment but in a contrasting mood

squeamishness: extreme sensitivity to anything unpleasant

the line she's been feeding to Mitch: the lies she has been telling Mitch

is no lily: is no virtuous innocent

plant: factory

"Say, it's only a paper moon": a popular song of the 1940s

slipped through her lily-white fingers: was lost by her. (The phrase 'lily-white fingers' reminds us of Stanley's earlier words, 'Sister Blanche is no lily', as well as mocking Blanche's uselessness)

goings-on: disreputable behaviour

Dame Blanche: Stanley uses the title sarcastically

showed here: showed up here, came here

Barnum and Bailey: a famous American circus founded in 1881; here the phrase is used to mean something artificial, unreal

pulled the wool over your eyes: deceived you

honky-tonk: description of the music of ragtime piano-playing, which is often heard in low-class bars

penny arcade: amusement arcade with coin-operated machines

put on her act: pretend

got wised up: discovered the truth

quit: left her

the same old lines: repeating the same lies

same old hooey: always the same old nonsense

the town was too small: she became too well known

loco – nuts: mad

washed up like poison: Blanche's immoral behaviour has now become known to everyone, just as poison separates from water and floats to the surface

visiting royalty: acting graciously like a royal personage on a visit

putting on all this act: pretending

"Out-of-Bounds": placed beyond the limits, forbidden to soldiers to visit

No, siree, Bob!:   emphatic colloquial form of denial

gotten mixed up with: became involved with, sexually or emotionally

high school superintendent: local government official supervising schools

called on the carpet: called in to be reprimanded

had her on the hook good and proper: caught her, leaving her no means of escape

she knew that the jig was all up: she knew that this was the end of her pretensions

practickly: practically

ordinance: law

Possess your soul in patience!: be patient! (a quotation from John Dryden's (1631–1700) poem *The Hind and the Panther* (1675), III, 839)

It's not my soul I'm worried about!: Stanley is hinting at Blanche's immorality

flighty: flirtatious

worshipped the ground he walked on: regarded him as God-like

degenerate: that is, homosexual. At this time homosexuality was generally thought to be unnatural and socially unacceptable

I'll stop at twenty-five: Blanche is of course several years older

company: visitors

buddy: close friend

outfit: army unit

through with her: no longer interested in her

wised up: in possession of all the facts

Blanche wouldn't go on a bus: Blanche would regard travelling by bus (coach) as vulgar

Period: full-stop; it is final

mapped out for her: fully decided for her

Toots: a term of endearment, here used mockingly

highball glass: tall glass for whisky and soda or a similar drink

The distant piano ... breakdown: the jarring piano music prophesies disaster

Scene VIII

The disastrous birthday supper has taken place without Mitch. Stella and Stanley sit in silence while Blanche chatters on with desperate gaiety. Reprimanded by his wife for his table manners, Stanley throws the crockery on the floor. He offers Blanche his birthday present, the bus ticket to Laurel. The shock is too much for her and she rushes off to the bathroom to be sick. Stella reproaches Stanley for his cruelty to her sister but while he defends himself she feels the first labour pains and asks to be taken to the hospital. They go out together, leaving Blanche on her own.

NOTES AND GLOSSARY:

empty lot: empty space which has not been built on
drawn: tense and tired-looking
stood up: kept waiting for someone who never comes
beau: admirer, boyfriend
cursed a blue streak: cursed shockingly, using bad language
front walk: front path to the house
making a pig of himself: eating greedily and messily
Huey Long: Huey Pierce Long (1893–1935), an American politician, Governor of Louisiana. Corrupt and a demagogue, he remained extremely popular with the poor for the work he did to improve the social services and reduce unemployment by a public works programme
stalks out: walks out stiffly
can make noise in the night: can make love noisily
get the coloured lights going: reach the full climax of sexual passion
lots of things could have happened: a number of things might have prevented Mitch from coming
Hydro-therapy: treatment of disease by bathing
without a nerve in your body: not nervous at all
proud as hell: very proud
wanta: want to
gonna: going to
Twenty-seven?: the questioning note shows that Stanley knows that she is much older than that
the Greyhound: a company operating long-distance coaches in the United States
The Varsouviana music: see notes on Scene VI; the polka tune, the motif of Blanche's tragedy, warns of disaster
gagging: retching, the sound of being sick
all that I took off her: the insults I accepted silently from her
Delicate piece: sensitive lady; Stanley is being ironical

I done nothing to no one: I have injured no-one. (The emphatic double
        negative is an ungrammatical form of speech)
I pulled you down off them columns ... going!: I brought you down to
        earth, to my level, with my love-making
showed: appeared
Hoity-toity: supercilious, haughty
with sinister rapidity: the quick polka tune is heard with a threatening
        rapidity
El pan de mais ...: (*Spanish*) maize bread without salt. (A snatch from a
        Mexican folk song which tells how God created man
        out of maize)

Scene IX

Later the same evening Blanche is sitting alone in the apartment; she
has been drinking steadily. Mitch arrives, unshaven and obviously drunk,
as well as hurt and angry. Blanche welcomes him flirtatiously but soon
realises that his attitude towards her has changed. He tells her bluntly that
he knows all about her, and Blanche, too despairing to lie, tries to explain
to him what had driven her to behave as she had done but Mitch does not
understand. He tries to rape her but she fights him off, threatening to raise
the alarm, and he leaves in confusion.

NOTES AND GLOSSARY:
robe: dressing-gown. (The scarlet colour may be symbolic,
        the scarlet woman is a whore)
the "Varsouviana": notice how the polka tune has taken over from the
        blue piano in this harrowing scene
Y'know: you know
uncavalier: unchivalrous
a cold shoulder: a deliberate show of indifference
a face like a thundercloud: an angry, threatening expression
uncouth apparel: rough work clothes
you dumb angel-puss: you stupid handsome man
plumps himself down: sits down heavily
I – haven't investigated: Blanche is lying, of course, pretending that she
        has not been drinking
Some things ... mine!: in claiming that the liquor is hers Blanche has
        contradicted her last statement
cross-examine the witness: ask searching questions as in a court of law
It always stops after that: we are made to realise that the music obsesses
        Blanche and that she is re-living the death of her
        husband over and over again in her mind
boxed out of your mind: stupid with drink

Southern Comfort: a well-known whisky-based liqueur
lapping it up: drinking it greedily
at the plant: at the factory
pitch: invented story
malarkey: nonsense
dished out: gave out as truth
straight: honest
put him in his place: made him realise that he was presuming, that he was my inferior socially
Rub-a-dub-dub ... tub!: the beginning of a nursery rhyme. Blanche is attempting to trivialise what Mitch is saying
Tarantula: a large tropical spider whose sting can kill
That's where I brought my victims: Blanche compares herself to a spider catching flies in a web. (We may also connect Blanche, who is a widow, with the female Black Widow spider which eats the male after they have mated)
intimacies: sexual relations
played out: finished, exhausted
gone up the water-spout: disappeared, was lost
have tied an old tin can ... kite: have brought me down to earth in a show of mockery
Flores para los muertos: (*Spanish*) flowers for the dead
The polka tune fades in: Blanche is reminded of her dead husband
Corones para los muertos: coronets for the dead, to decorate graves; there is a strong cult of death in Mexico
blood-stained pillow-slips "... changing": Blanche is remembering in snatches the terrible years of looking after dying relatives
paddy-wagon: police van taking those arrested to the police station
The polka music fades away: the past fades away, leaving Blanche with the bitter present
not clean enough: not respectable enough
The distant piano is slow and blue: the sad New Orleans music returns

Scene X

It is several hours later the same night. Blanche has been drinking and is now trying to pack her belongings. Confused and drunk, she has put on an evening gown and her cheap tiara. Stanley arrives, a little drunk as well. The baby will not be born for some hours yet and he has come home to snatch some sleep. Blanche pretends that she has had a telegram from an old admirer and is packing to go on a Caribbean cruise. She also claims that Mitch had called to apologise for his behaviour and that she sent him away. Stanley denounces her pitiful fantasies quite bluntly as lies. Excited by Blanche's evident terror, he overpowers her and rapes her.

NOTES AND GLOSSARY:

brilliants: fake jewels cut with many surfaces to make them sparkle

the rhinestone tiara: the tiara that Stanley had pulled out of her trunk in Scene II

spectral: ghostly

a moonlight swim at the old rock quarry: in her mind Blanche is at the Belle Reve of her girlhood, surrounded by her reckless young admirers

the honky-tonk music: the loud, garish tune sets the tone for the nightmare scene that follows

a little shut-eye: a little sleep

fine feathers: fine clothes

A fireman's ball: a dance organised by the local fire brigade, a proverbial cheap, humble entertainment

What do you know?: who would have expected it? (Stanley is being heavily ironic)

a bolt from the blue: a thunderbolt out of a clear sky, i.e. something totally unexpected

ATO pin: Auxiliary Territorial Officer pin. (For the significance of pins see notes on Scene IV)

Biscayne Boulevard: a street in Miami

relic: something from the past

Tiffany: a famous New York jeweller

Dallas: second largest city in Texas, the centre of the oil industry

where gold spouts from the ground: where wealth comes from the oil-wells

company: visitors

geyser: upward stream of liquid

bury the hatchet: stop fighting

loving-cup: cup passed round at the end of a feast, to be drunk from by all as a token of friendship

a red letter night: a special night, a night to remember and celebrate

break out: take out of its wrappings

put on the dog: dress up in one's best clothes

any: in any way

casting my pearls before swine: wasting my special gifts on people who do not appreciate them (see the Bible, Matthew 7:6, 'neither cast ye your pearls before swine')

Swine, huh?: Stanley does not recognise the biblical quotation and sees the phrase as another personal insult

gave him his walking papers: ordered him to leave

Mardi Gras: Mardi Gras carnival celebrated in New Orleans on Shrove Tuesday, the day before Lent, the period of repentance in the Christian calendar, begins. It is known for its extravagant costumes

rag-picker: man who buys old clothes

pull any wool over this boy's eyes: deceive me

the Queen of the Nile: Cleopatra, Queen of Egypt, a celebrated beauty of the ancient world

jiggles the hook: moves the receiver-rest up and down to call the operator

sinuously: in an undulating, snake-like manner

rolled: robbed

rooting: searching

Western Union: a large telephone company in the United States

left th' phone off th' hook: haven't replaced the receiver

"blue piano": there is growing menace in the piano music now

interfere with you: molest you sexually

The inhuman jungle voices rise up: the stage directions aim to create a nightmare on the stage

putting on: pretending, putting on an act

So you want some rough-house!: so you want violence (to heighten the sexual experience)

We've had this date: this was meant to happen. (In a way Stanley is right; the tension between them had always had sexual overtones, as Blanche's awareness of Stanley's coarse masculinity dictated her behaviour towards him)

Scene XI

The last scene takes place some weeks later. Stanley and his friends are playing poker again (though Stanley alone acts in a normal way, his friends are too distressed by what they know is happening to concentrate on the game). Stella is packing Blanche's things while Blanche is having another bath. She believes that she is going on a cruise with her admirer but in reality she has been committed to a mental hospital by her sister. As Stella cannot accept Blanche's story of the rape and go on living with her husband, she has decided to regard her sister as mentally unstable. The doctor and matron of the hospital arrive and Blanche, realising the truth at last, tries to escape. The doctor's gentle courtesy calms her down and she leaves with him quietly. Stella is distressed, sobbing with grief and remorse, but Stanley's caresses soothe her to accept his love-making.

NOTES AND GLOSSARY:

Sound of water can be heard: Blanche is having yet another bath. (It might be said that her passion for bathing is an expression of her longing to be pure again)

raw: harsh

lurid: ghastly, threatening

Drew to an inside straight and made it: took a risk, aimed at a perfect winning hand and was successful

Maldita sea tu suerto!: *(Spanish)* damn your luck!

greaseball: a term of abuse for someone of Latin-American origin, especially a Mexican. It is a reference to both the rich, oily food and the Latins' allegedly oily complexion

prodigiously: wonderfully, greatly

Salerno: port in the heel of southern Italy, the scene of fierce fighting during the Second World War

rat-race: struggle for survival at the expense of others

You ... bull: Mitch is so upset by Stanley's behaviour and his treatment of Blanche that he has become inarticulate

Brag: speak boastfully of yourself in an arrogant manner

bull: a reference to Stanley's blatant coarse masculinity as well as to his boastful talk

bouclé: silk material with looped threads making an uneven surface

I couldn't believe her story ... living with Stanley: in other words Stella chose to pretend that her sister was mad, rather than face the reality of her husband's behaviour

Della Robbia blue: an intense blue used by the Italian artist Luca della Robbia (*c.* 1400–82) for the background of his medaillons and reliefs

blue of the robe: traditionally the Virgin Mary is dressed in blue

Are these grapes washed?: again the insistence on cleansing and purity

the only clean thing in the Quarter: the same obsession again

quinine: medicine from cinchona bark, used against malaria and high fever generally

a clean white sack: once more an insistence on purity

MATRON: woman in charge of nursing in a hospital or a similar institution

The "Varsouviana" faintly plays: the faint music signals the rising fear in Blanche's mind

My silver toilet articles: a silver-backed hairbrush, clothes-brush and a silver comb. These articles are remnants of Blanche and Stella's privileged background

Please don't get up: a reminder of the incident in Scene III

The "Varsouviana" is playing distantly: the presence of the Varsouviana increases with the terror Blanche feels

Lurid reflections . . . noises of the jungle: the stage directions repeat the images in the setting for the rape in Scene X. Thus, both actions in which the terrified Blanche is violated, are linked

Doc: short for 'Doctor'

fire-bell: alarm-bell warning of a fire, a harsh, ominous sound

Madre de Dios . . . muy mala!: (*Spanish*) Mother of God! A bad business, very, very bad!

Quit the blubber!:   stop crying!

this bone-headed cry-baby: this stupid, childishly emotional man

take it easy!:   don't get excited!

pinions her arms: holds her arms firmly to her sides

These fingernails . . . trimmed: once institutionalised, Blanche will not be allowed to let her fingernails grow long, for her own safety as well as that of the asylum staff

Jacket: a straitjacket, a canvas contraption for controlling the violently insane

EUNICE *descends . . . her arms*: as Blanche exits, Stella and Stanley's baby is brought in. It is a symbol of the death of one generation and an old-fashioned culture and the birth of a new breed of American, of a new life force

luxurious: pleasantly self-indulgent

voluptuously: in a voice hinting at sexual pleasure, which accompanies his caress of his wife's breasts

the "blue piano" and the muted trumpet: the play closes with the music of New Orleans, its easy acceptance of passion and suffering

Part 3

Commentary

Structure and technique

The structure of a play or a novel is the framework on which the writer builds his work. Structure matters because the basic shape of a work will dictate its form and perhaps impose some decisive limitations on the writer's imagination. In a play there are a number of practical considerations which will affect its structure. First of all its length is dictated by the attention span of the audience, the time for which the spectators are prepared to remain in their seats and give their full attention to what is happening on the stage.

There have been some plays of exceptional length, for instance some parts of Shakespeare's history plays, such as the two parts of *Henry IV* and parts 1–3 of *Henry VI*, if they are performed together, as is sometimes the case. Among modern plays Eugene O'Neill's (1889–1953) *Long Day's Journey into Night* and his *The Iceman Cometh* exceed the usual length of a play. But the spectators tend to regard performances of unusual length as more of a sporting challenge or endurance test than an aesthetic experience, and such productions are rare.

Another practical consideration is that of the setting. Constant changes of scenery mean constant interruptions of the action and a considerable additional burden on the cost of the production. These considerations were of much less importance in early drama, where scenery was not used, and are less important once more today when naturalistic scenery is quite out of fashion, and settings can be created by ingenious use of sophisticated lighting. Nevertheless the tradition of limiting the changes of scenery is by now well established and convenient to follow.

The convention of imposing rules on playwrights has a very long history indeed. These rules, the so-called three unities (of time, space and action) had been wrongly attributed by the literary critics of the Renaissance to the Greek philosopher and critic Aristotle (384–322BC) who merely described the characteristic features of some Greek tragedies, without formulating any rules. Though the unities do not go back to ancient Greece, they have been observed – and broken, most notably by Shakespeare – since the fifteenth century. Roughly speaking, the unity of time demanded that the time span of the action taking place on the stage should not exceed twenty-four hours, while the unity of space stipulated that the setting of the play should remain the same throughout. Less easy to define was the third of the unities, that of action. It required that the action should be complete, centring on the main characters, and that the events represented should be relevant to the main plot and offer the audience a satisfying whole.

Though it must be said that the unities were taken more seriously by literary theoreticians than by the dramatists themselves, nevertheless they were – and still are – considered and followed, if only as a rough guide. Other considerations developed for practical reasons: thus the audience's attention span, mentioned above, influenced the division of a play into acts, normally three or five in number (often with subdivisions into scenes) which allowed for changes of mood as well as facilitating the change of scenery and of the characters present on the stage.

If we turn to *A Streetcar Named Desire* we shall find that Williams paid a good deal of attention, consciously or unconsciously, to the unities. (We should remember that in his student days at the University of Missouri and at Washington University he read avidly, gaining a thorough knowledge of the nineteenth-century dramatists, founders of modern drama, notably Strindberg, Ibsen and Chekhov.) In *A Streetcar Named Desire* the unity of space is certainly adhered to, as all of the action takes place either in the Kowalskis' apartment or in the street just outside it. The action, however, is not confined within twenty-four hours. Most of the play takes place within a few days in May, the climax follows after an interval of three months, and its grim aftermath some weeks later. Yet we are not aware of any diffusion of action, so swiftly and naturally do the events follow one another. The protagonists' characteristics and sentiments are established quite quickly, and there is a feeling of speedy movement forward to an inescapable conclusion.

For the ancient Greek dramatists a tragedy was the representation of the fall of a good man, brought about by a flaw in his character (known as *hamartia*). Though Blanche DuBois can hardly be described as a good woman in conventional terms, yet the destruction of her hopes for peace and security, her final descent into madness, and our awareness of the fate in store for her call forth those emotions of pity and terror which the Greek dramatists sought to inspire in their audiences. It is her fate that concerns us primarily and here lies the unity of action of the play. The author is urging us to concern ourselves with her first and foremost, since she is the only character in the play who appears in every scene, and also the only character whose past and future are reasonably well established by the end of the play. By contrast we learn very little about Stanley's background. (Are his Polish parents alive or dead? What are his feelings about them? The only family connection he mentions, in Scene X, is the cousin who could open bottles with his teeth.) We know that he fought in the Second World War, at Salerno, and apparently did well in the army, gaining the rank of Master Sergeant. We are left almost as much in the dark about

Stella. Nothing is said of her life since she left home, and very little about the reasons for her departure.

Blanche's presence in every scene ensures the continuity of the action. A curious structural characteristic of Williams's play is that instead of the conventional division into acts it is simply a sequence of eleven scenes. Moreover, each of these eleven scenes might be regarded almost as a complete one-act playlet, ending in a dramatic climax. There is a certain amount of repetition of actions and speeches, with significant variations (see, for instance, Blanche's accounts of her marriage in Scenes I, II, VI and IX), as Blanche interacts with the other characters in the play. These repetitions, and their variations, serve to add to our understanding of the characters. We might also remember here that Williams wrote a number of one-act plays over the years, and may well have found it easier to present a single dramatic incident than to carry the plot through the conventional number of acts.

There is another way of looking at the unusual structure of *A Streetcar Named Desire*. The smooth sequence of the scenes, with no formal breaks in the form of acts, makes the play seem more like a film. We are all cinema goers and television viewers nowadays, and find it easy to accept the structure of this play. Williams undoubtedly took a great interest in the cinema from his youth: remember that he acted as film critic for his high school magazine, and that at the beginning of his career as a dramatist he was hired by MGM as a scriptwriter. He wrote only one script (entitled *The Gentleman Caller*), and it was rejected because of its Southern setting (even after the phenomenal success of *Gone with the Wind* in 1939, MGM executives still believed that films set in the American South were box office failures). The rejection is only important because Williams made use of the script to write his first successful full-length play, *The Glass Menagerie*. It should be mentioned that the play was divided into seven scenes rather than the conventional number of acts, thus first establishing the structure used in *A Streetcar Named Desire*. It may be that this was an approach taken over from the original film script, because Williams found it congenial. Equally he may have been influenced, consciously or unconsciously, by films when writing the play. Whatever its provenance, the structure suited Williams, and so he adopted it again in *A Streetcar Named Desire*, and later in *Camino Real*, divided into sixteen 'Blocks'.

In this context we might find a comment made by the American playwright Arthur Miller interesting. In discussing *The Glass Menagerie* he speaks of Williams's 'rhapsodic insistence that form serve his utterance rather than dominating and cramping it', and the same might be said of *A Streetcar Named Desire*. The sequence of short scenes may be seen as stressing the inexorable movement forward to a catastrophe, making use of the form to emphasise the content of the play.

Mention was made above of the influence the structure of a work exercises on its form. In *A Streetcar Named Desire* the sequence of relatively short scenes requires a rapid build-up to the climax with which each scene/playlet ends. The music, whether the 'blue piano' or the 'Varsouviana' polka, is employed to establish a mood quickly, and the precise stage directions with their sharp visual detail serve the same purpose. Williams's apprenticeship in the film industry, however short-lived, may have played its part in this intensely visual approach to the play. If you study his stage directions you will quickly notice that they are concerned with more than simply descriptions of the settings and the entrances and exits of the players. They seem to paint pictures with words, and, incidentally, they contain some of the best writing in the play. They are concerned with impressions and emotions more than with realism.

The close of each scene is remarkable as well; we are presented with an almost wordless *tableau vivant*, with the actors frozen in dramatic poses as if in a cinema still (remember for instance Blanche's sudden and unexpected collapse at the end of Scene I, or Stanley's triumphant grin over Stella's head at the end of Scene IV). Any words spoken have a weightiness, a significance designed to attract the audience's attention. Blanche's 'The blind are – leading the blind' (Scene II), her 'I need kindness now' (Scene III) or 'Sometimes – there's God – so quickly!' (Scene VI), all have this dramatic effect.

The music – both the 'blue piano' and the polka tune – is used in a way strongly reminiscent of the cinema. It prepares the audience for a dramatic scene, heightening the mood and acting in parallel with actors on stage.

If *A Streetcar Named Desire* has features reminiscent of the cinema, this quality of Williams's stagecraft was not lost on Hollywood. It is an astonishing fact that no fewer than fifteen of his plays were made into films, with the author collaborating on the scripts for seven of them. To some extent this was due to their evident adaptability for the screen, as well as to their intrinsic merit, and to Williams's fame and his public appeal. The absence of the conventional division into acts was a plus when turning the play into a film. Moreover, Williams's plays shared with the cinema a readiness to integrate scenes of violence and sexual passion into the action. Though he came to regret his shock tactics, and claimed that he employed them to drive home a moral lesson, his style was still good box office material. His dialogue was usually simple, his dramatic instinct very strong and his delight in sensationalism notorious.

Themes

Passion and fate

Quite often the title of a play will tell the audience what to expect from the play: think of Arthur Miller's *Death of a Salesman*, G. B. Shaw's *Saint*

Joan or Shakespeare's *The Taming of a Shrew*, to name a few, very much at random.

Williams's unusual and memorable title hints at the play's main themes with an intriguing obliqueness. A streetcar moving along the rails to its destination and unable to change its course is a fitting symbol of a relentless inevitability, of a fate which cannot be avoided. The metaphor is elaborated further in the streetcar's destination – Desire. Desire, or sexual passion, is the moving force that carries the heroine of Williams's play to her fate. In Scene IV the DuBois sisters admit their submission to sexual desire in the very same metaphor:

> BLANCHE: What you are talking about is brutal desire – just – Desire! –
> the name of that rattle-trap street-car that bangs through the
> Quarter, up one old narrow street and down another . . .
> STELLA: Haven't you ever ridden on that streetcar?
> BLANCHE: It brought me here . . .

Not stated directly in the title, but implicit in Blanche's first comment on her arrival ('They told me to take a street-car named Desire, and then to transfer to one called Cemeteries and . . . get off at – Elysian Fields!') is another major theme of the play, death, which is the inevitable destination of those who follow their passions, blindly. Williams was quite aware of the full symbolic potential of the title of his play. When he was living in New Orleans in 1946 and working on *A Streetcar Named Desire*, he wrote in an essay about two streetcars near where he was living, one called 'Desire' and the other called 'Cemeteries': 'Their indiscourageable progress up and down Royal Street struck me as having some symbolic bearing of a broad nature on the life in the Vieux Carré – and everywhere else, for that matter.'[1]

The helplessness of the individual against the fate that is foreordained by his or her nature and weaknesses of character is also symbolised by the image of the moth, so fatally attracted to the flame of passion. On her entrance in Scene I the stage directions describe Blanche as resembling a moth and throughout the play she is seen as being drawn closer and closer to bright lights with a mixture of terror and fascination. Blanche's tragedy is that she realises her fate (she says that she has to wear 'the colours of butterfly wings' (Scene V) in order to survive) but is powerless to avoid it.

Williams himself seems to have been convinced that there is a predestination of a sort at work in people's lives; that by standing back and examining one's own past one could trace influences at work from the earliest childhood, shaping one's character which then will inexorably steer the course of one's life. As if to stress his conception of the individual as a passive victim, he himself let events direct him throughout his life. There were periods when he drifted (usually after periods of hectic

[1]Quoted by Donald Spoto, *The Kindness of Strangers* (1985), p. 129.

activity), moving aimlessly from city to city, from state to state in the United States, from country to country in Europe or Asia. His drifting went deeper than simply moving from place to place: he drifted emotionally, from one short-lived affair to another, ever refusing to make a relationship permanent and to commit himself to another person. Like Blanche he was dependent on the kindness of strangers, and, like Blanche perhaps, he was unable to change the pattern of his behaviour. Brief affairs that satisfied a physical need only could of course be conducted with strangers, leaving his essential self untouched. In Blanche's case, her past is spoken of in hints only (or in Stanley's crude innuendos), and we remain in ignorance about her emotional life as distinct from her sexual escapades. It seems, however, that the tragic death of her husband left her emotionally crippled and doomed to remain alone. A deep unease, an awareness of something missing, pervaded Williams's life as it did Blanche's. Though he was probably unaware of this at a conscious level, his frantic urge to write may have been an expression of this unease, of a lack of purpose and meaning in his life. (Again we may draw a parallel with Blanche whose restlessness and bright chatter seem to emphasise the underlying unease.) Only while he was writing could Williams feel that he was working towards some purpose, and only in his work, even if it was of poor quality, as was often the case in his later years, did he exist.

Let us not forget, either, Stella's blind passion for her husband, which leads her to choose Stanley's physical love rather than the ugly truth of her sister's rape, thus sealing Blanche's tragic fate. The two themes are inextricably joined then, as they are in the title of the play – the force that propels us, our fate, is sexual passion. It has been suggested that *A Streetcar Named Desire* is a coded autobiography, an act of confession: unable to speak openly of his homosexuality, which was then still illegal, Williams used Blanche as his mouthpiece. In support of this theory it could be argued that the homosexuality of Blanche's husband is a manifestation of the author's compulsion to bring in the forbidden subject. Blanche might have equally well accused her husband in public if she had caught him in bed with a woman (though of course such an escapade would never have carried the same stigma). Perhaps, but Williams liked to shock his audience for dramatic effect, and homosexuality was deeply shocking then. Also, such a discovery could certainly have had a permanent, shattering effect on the young wife, accounting for the turn her life took afterwards.

And yet, is it necessary to speak of coded meanings here? Sexual passion takes various forms, and Blanche's nymphomania is perhaps not so very different from the homosexual urges that drove Williams to such excesses. The writer had first-hand knowledge of physical desire and so could sympathise with his heroine. Clearly, it is not the form that matters but the intensity and recklessly destructive nature of the passion.

Death

Linked to the themes of the inevitability of fate and of the destructiveness of passion is the third theme of the play, that of death. Williams was obsessed with the gruesome reality of death and this preoccupation finds expression in the play in Blanche's speech justifying the loss of Belle Reve by all the deaths in the family and the expenses of dying. Her descriptions are oblique, but no less horrifying for that – the woman so swollen with disease that she could not be fitted into a coffin, but 'had to be burned like rubbish', the death rattle, the struggle for breath (Scene I), the blood-stained pillowcases that she herself had to change because there were no longer the servants to do it (Scene IX). In contrast to Blanche's descriptions of the horrors of dying, in her conversation with Mitch (Scene VI) any references to his mother's approaching death ('When she passes on') are indirect and genteel. The contrast is deliberate, of course, and is used to stress the difference in their backgrounds and attitudes.

As well as dwelling on death in descriptions Williams employs a symbolic figure of death, the Mexican seller of tin flowers for decorating coffins and graves (Scene X). Like some of the stage directions in Scenes X and XI (*'lurid reflections'* and *'inhuman voices like cries in a jungle'*) she is an example of the Expressionist element in the play, that is, an attempt on the part of the playwright to convey outwardly what is occurring within the minds of the characters.

At the back of Blanche's mind, and manifested in the polka music, is the memory of her husband's suicide. His tragic death is at first only dimly perceived by the audience, but gradually, as the truth becomes known, we see his death ever more clearly as the obvious, acceptable explanation of Blanche's instability. That Williams was terrified of dying is amply documented in the recollections of his friends. His hypochondria grew into a dangerous, life-threatening obsession, but it had probably always been there, right from his childhood. Its roots were to be found in the serious childhood illness (diphtheria) which nearly killed him, and in the over-protective care lavished on him by his mother during his illness and long convalescence.

Madness

Hand and hand with his fear of death went Williams's fear of madness. Of course its roots too lay in family history, mainly in his beloved sister's fate. He blamed himself for being absent during the crucial time and so allowing the lobotomy performed on Rose to take place (quite unnecessarily in the light of present-day practice and research). It may also be assumed as a matter of course that he was afraid that Rose's mental instability was hereditary, and that he watched himself agonisingly for any symptoms of madness. He never forgave his brother for having him committed to hospital when he was at the brink of death from excessive drinking and drug-taking. In Williams's eyes his brother turned a nightmare into horrible reality, and tried to give him the same fate that Rose had had.

In this way Williams knew from his own experience Blanche's fears, her constant awareness of a slipping of controls, of a temptation to let go. All the classic symptoms are there – the fits of embarrassingly forced gaiety, the sudden panic, the withdrawal into unreality and – as for Williams himself – the need for alcohol as a way to avoid thinking and remembering.

The threat of madness to Blanche is apparent from the very first scene: 'as you may have noticed – I'm *not* very *well* . . .' Clearly, she herself is also aware of the fragility of her mental state. At first she relies on alcohol to keep this knowledge at bay, but as the play progresses and Stanley's treatment of her becomes increasingly abusive, she retreats into a fantasy world of romantic songs and soft lighting. This can be seen as an initial stage in her madness, in which she creates her own reality in order to remove herself from a world with which she cannot cope. When the memories of the past and the harsh forces of the present (represented by Stanley) become too powerful, her phony reality is shattered and is re-placed by another form of madness. The world she sees in Scene XI is, like her fantasy world, a distorted version of reality, but whereas that world was pleasant and reassuring, this is brutal and menacing. The stage is full of weird contorted sounds and lights and we, the audience, have suddenly been propelled into the landscape of Blanche's mind. Thus the final reversion to the normality of life as she is led from the stage is particularly shocking and effective.

Other themes

There are other themes in the play, linked to the main ones discussed above. The train which roars along the L & N tracks is a dramatic device which is linked with Stanley. Both the train and Stanley are products of a dynamic, modern America and they are at odds with the old Southern life that Blanche represents. Furthermore they both contribute in some way to her downfall; in Scene IV the train's noise enables Stanley to eavesdrop on the sisters' conversation and in Scene X it renders Blanche petrified with fear just before Stanley attacks and rapes her. We might also contrast this loud, aggressive locomotive with the rattling, old-fashioned streetcar in the same way that we contrast the conflicting worlds of Stanley and Blanche.

Much is made of the theme of light. Speaking of her first love, Blanche describes it as a 'blinding light', which was turned off again when her husband died 'and never for one moment since has there been any light that's stronger than this – kitchen – candle . . .' (Scene VI). Her present fear of strong light is explained by Mitch quite prosaically in Scene IX as a reluctance to submit her face to close scrutiny and so reveal her real age, but equally it can be seen in symbolic terms as part of her inability to face reality, of her need to dress it up in the pretty colours of the reality she creates for herself – which other people see as lying. As she says, speaking sadly of the short life of the birthday candles, 'wind blows them out and after that happens, electric light bulbs go on and you see too plainly' (Scene VIII). There is the overt symbolism of the paper lantern which she asks Mitch to fit over a naked light bulb to hide its ugliness and which he rips off during the confrontation in Scene IX. In Scene X Stanley too refers to it slightingly as yet another of Blanche's pretensions, and rips it off yet again in triumph at the moment of Blanche's final defeat in Scene XI.

As a final point, we might consider the images conjured up by the names of the two sisters. Blanche DuBois, loosely translated from the French, means 'white woods'. It is a name lodged in a romantic past and is fitting for a woman who is to become increasingly obsessed with purity and virginity. By contrast, not only is Stella's name associated with the fire and light that her sister fears ('Stella for Star!' – Scene I) but whereas Blanche has kept her maiden name she has dropped hers and embraced the name of her New American husband.

The American South

Any discussion of *A Streetcar Named Desire* is bound to touch on the nostalgic theme of the American South. Although Blanche might be seen as an embodiment of the old plantation culture, in contrast to the crude vitality of the immigrant New American, Stanley, there is very little romantic glorification of the South in this play. Stanley mentions the mansion of Belle Reve with its columns, but only to boast how he brought Stella down from those columns to his own level. Blanche's recollections are too painfully raw to allow her to forget the reality of Belle Reve in poverty, amidst physical suffering and the squalor of death. She seems reluctant to speak of it, perhaps because she too had been instrumental in its fall.

We must remember that Williams's mother, Edwina, certainly looked back with nostalgia on her girlhood, when she was the pretty, popular daughter of an esteemed clergyman, and that she complained to her children about her demeaning position as the wife of an insignificant employee of a shoe company in St Louis. She conveyed to her children her own idealised picture of Southern society, and when in adulthood Williams turned against her, blaming her for all his problems, he perhaps turned against the romanticised South as well. Certainly in *The Glass Menagerie* he mocks in the character of Amanda Wingfield not only his mother's stifling possessiveness and insensitivity, but also her pretensions as a Southern belle. In the circumstances it would have been only natural for Williams to see the Southern myth as a pretentious lie in which he was not prepared to collude.

And yet, though he will not paint an idealised picture of it, he found Southern society attractive in its insistence on cultural values, on beauty and loyalty. Blanche, the Southern belle given to quoting lines of poetry, stands against Stanley, the coarse, materialistic man of modern America. Their antagonism is not only sexual tension, it embodies a clash of opposing cultural values as well.

In the end Williams is still a Southern writer, declaring 'I write out of love of the South . . . (which) once had a way of life that I am just old enough to remember – a culture that had grace, elegance, an inbred culture, not a society based on money.'[1] The contradictions of his attitudes become the dramatic tensions of opposites in his play.

Language

In a discussion of the language of Williams's play it is useful to recall that in a letter to the English drama critic Kenneth Tynan[2] he described his writing as 'lyric', and that Brook Atkinson's 1947 review of *A Streetcar Named Desire* in the *New York Times* speaks of Williams as 'a genuinely poetic playwright'. Yet Longman's *Dictionary of Literary Terms* defines a lyric as 'poetry which is neither narrative nor dramatic', 'expressing in a personal manner the feelings and thoughts of an individual speaker (not necessarily the poet)'.

At first we may find it difficult to reconcile *A Streetcar Named Desire* with its largely naturalistic plot and its emphasis on dramatic effects with the two estimates of its author's main strength quoted above. But perhaps we should look beyond the form and towards the author's purpose in writing the play. In it he expresses, obliquely at times, emotions and passions he himself felt strongly. His characters, Blanche apart, may speak haltingly and ungrammatically, but the tide of emotion that sweeps through the play, through the events to which we are witness, speaks beyond words in the language of high passion. It is worth remembering this even as we consider the words the individual characters speak.

The language of a play is of course of greatest importance. What the characters say is the only means the playwright has at hand for shaping them into distinctive personages. In a novel the writer's authorial voice can influence our perception of the characters without their opening their

[1]Quoted by Donald Spoto, *op. cit.*, p. 139, from an article by Louise Davis, 'That Baby Doll Man', *Nashville Tennessee Magazine*, 3 March 1957.
[2]Quoted by Patricia Hern in the Methuen Student Edition of the play, p. xliii.

mouths once. In a play, by contrast, a characters' words and actions (as interpreted by the actor, of course) are all that the playwright has to give them life.

Williams takes a good deal of trouble over the speech of the protagonists of *A Streetcar Named Desire*. Blanche's personality is established very quickly with her cool dismissal of Eunice. More of it is revealed in her first greeting of her sister ('Stella for Star!') with its rather forced poetic note. We soon discover that such highflown expressions are natural to her and, moreover, that they are not necessarily false. Her yearning for beauty, for delicacy, is true – but of course she is also driven by other, opposing urges. The girlish flirtatiousness she displays towards Stanley and Mitch, with its overtones of vulgarity, is not just the style of a fading beauty striving to recapture her lost youth; it is also part of her sexual armoury. Her coy lady-like phrases are open invitations ('May I have a drag on your cig?' – Scene II), presumably perfected in her escapades in Laurel, and are a sharp reminder of her past.

Blanche's use of quotations serves to remind us that she is, after all, a well-read teacher of English, but they also tell us of her true love for poetry. She breaks into genuine poetical speech when she is deeply moved and trying to express her emotions faithfully, as in her oblique justification of her past behaviour in Scene V, or in the light images describing her love for her husband and his death (Scene VI). The authoritarianism of the classroom teacher is heard when she is rebuking Stella for her untidiness in Scene I, or giving her instructions about her toilette in the last scene ('See if it's crushed . . . Try and locate a bunch of artificial violets . . .'). The striking variations in the style and syntax of her speeches, ranging from a cool business-like tone (as when handing over to Stanley the file on Belle Reve in Scene II) to the disjointed jumble of panic-stricken appeals to the telephone operator (Scene X), signal to the audience the precariousness of her mental stability. If we listen (or read) carefully we can form a clear picture of Blanche, and find in her words a confirmation of Stanley's later allegations, as well as an advance warning of her probable fate.

The way Stanley speaks is equally revealing. His ungrammatical speech tells of his lack of formal education ('I never was a very good English student' – Scene I), as does his naïve harping on the Napoleonic Code in Scene II, which betrays the uneducated man's belief in the magic power of words. His lavatorial jokes and crude language spell out the coarseness in his character and he uses them to express his dislike of Blanche's gentility. On his own ground, however, he has confidence and a kind of dignity, whether criticising the garage mechanics or discussing his bowling team. There is never any doubt in our minds that he is the leader of the pack among his card-playing cronies and, interestingly, when they speak of him and to him they betray not only their respect and fear of him, but some affection as well. He is unsure of himself socially and quick to take offence for any social insult (thus, betraying his ignorance of the Bible, he takes Blanche's reference to casting pearls before swine to be an insult aimed specifically at him, the Polish pig – Scene X). The one flash of poetical language, his description of sexual ecstasy as coloured lights, is all the more striking as his language is generally pedestrian. It is effective dramatically, and convincingly expresses his passion for his wife. His revelations of Blanche's past in Scene VII are illuminating. Some of his jaunty phrases (referring to Blanche as 'Dame Blanche', using the jocular affirmation 'No, siree, Bob!') are no doubt an expression of his triumph over his enemy, but equally they are used to cover his unease. He must be aware of the effect his investigations will have, not only on the blissfully ignorant Blanche but on his wife as well. The niceties of behaviour towards women are not a part of his code, which acknowledges loyalty to men only, but he is uneasy nevertheless, and his language shows it.

Stella presents a very different case. Her speech is mostly restrained and practical, as befits someone who has made her way on her own, turning her back on her upbringing, and necessarily suppressing some emotions at least. She grows weary of Blanche's vanity which requires constant reassurance but she controls her irritation well. Her self-discipline enables her to live in peace with her neighbours but there is an intrinsic contrast between her matter-of-fact, restrained way of speaking and her passionate love for her husband which makes her accept the run-down house and the rowdy, vulgar neighbours. In the end cool reasoning makes her betray her sister, dismissing her sister's story of the rape as a lie. She has moral scruples ('I don't know if I did the right thing' – Scene XI) but reasons her way out of them.

The fourth of the chief players, Mitch, presents no problems for Williams. A deeply conventional, timid person, he speaks almost exclusively in prosaic clichés ('Poker shouldn't be played in a house with women – Scene III; 'A man with a heavy build has got to be careful' – Scene VI). His plodding conversations with Blanche are entertaining because she responds to his prosing by using language even more cliché-ridden, amusing herself by presenting herself as the sort of girl she is sure Mitch would wish for. Thus when he speaks not of sweat but, in a genteel way, of perspiration, she responds with a cliché about perspiration being healthy. Language alone suffices to sketch out Mitch's character for us, setting him aside as humourless, ineffectual, a loser.

There is another voice to be heard in the play, that is, the wordless voice of music. Both the 'blue piano' and the polka tune which only Blanche (and the audience) can hear are more than background music. The 'blue piano' certainly sets the mood of a scene, but it acts as a warning or a cry of triumph as well, while the polka has a specific function, emphasised by the fact that only Blanche can hear it (and that it always stops with the sound of a shot). It is a wordless musical replay of the nightmare in her mind. It is also significant perhaps that the 'blue piano' is the voice of New Orleans, modern, bold, brash, strident at times, while the polka, originating in the Old World of Europe, is the old-fashioned dance music of the formal ballrooms of Southern society. The two tunes may also be seen as representing the clash of the new order with the old. The popular songs that Blanche likes to sing in her bath (mocked by Stanley's 'Some canary-bird, huh!' – Scene VII) have a dramatic function too, their pathetic sentimentality presenting an ironic contrast with Stanley's revelations of Blanche's murky past, which go on next door.

The lyricism which Williams saw in his writing perhaps emerges most clearly in the stage directions. For the readers of the play the 'detailed description of Elysian Fields, of its sights, sounds and smells is enormously effective in creating in our minds this run-down area of New Orleans. We can easily *'feel the warm breath of the brown river'*, smell the *'faint redolences of bananas and coffee'* and hear *'the infatuated fluency of brown fingers'* playing the *'blue piano'* in the first description of Scene I. The characterisation of Stanley as 'the gaudy seed-bearer' is not only a skilful summing-up, it is also a snatch of poetry. At times it almost seems as if Williams the lyricist, hemmed in by the exigencies of a more or less realistic plot, feels free to burst out joyfully in his stage directions, where he can use his own poetic voice.

Characters

Blanche DuBois

For those who are familiar with the 1951 film version of the play it is difficult to distinguish between the heroine of Williams's play and Vivien Leigh's portrayal. However, it is salutary to remember that originally Williams wrote the part for another actress, Tallulah Bankhead, and that Jessica Tandy (and later Uta Hagen) played her in the first staging of the play. By general agreement it is a plum part, such as all actresses dream of.

Blanche is without a doubt Williams's greatest creation, a character that has taken on life beyond the play, inviting speculation on her fate, as we see her leave on the courteous doctor's arm, ignorant (though apprehensive) of the hideous fate that awaits her. She clearly engaged her creator's imagination as well: he remarked later that she had always been a survivor and that he was sure that she would make a full recovery in the asylum, and go on to marry her 'Gentleman Caller'.

This surprising speculation underlines the complexity of Blanche's character. On her entrance in Scene I we see her as a delicate, moth-like creature, looking *'as if she were arriving at a summer tea or cocktail party in the garden district'*. She is *'daintily dressed'* in an immaculate white suit, with white gloves and hat, and presents a picture of genteel purity.

This is a deliberate strategy on the playwright's part, of course, preparing the ground for the shocking revelations of Blanche's past to have their full effect. We soon receive a warning of what is to come when Blanche, waiting in the apartment, discovers a bottle of whisky as if by instinct. She quickly drinks a half-tumblerful, washes out the glass and replaces the bottle. This is the behaviour of the secret drinker and we are meant to take note of it, even though we discover only by degrees what it is that Blanche is trying to forget by drinking.

The first meeting of the sisters contributes further to our understanding of Blanche. Her affected cry of 'Stella for Star!' strikes a false note; again, only gradually do we realise that the affected poses and exaggerated, emotional phrases are in fact entirely genuine within the imaginary reality of her mind. It is a part of Blanche's character that she must overstate feelings to fit in with this reality. The point to be stressed here is that not only ugly, distressing facts have to be dressed up in this way: the whole of Blanche's life is given over to play-acting, not only out of necessity but for its own sake. The rare moments when she speaks the plain unvarnished truth, without dramatising it, are jarring and shocking.

Although she pretends most of the time, we are aware of the fear beneath the brittle chatter. There is always a threat of hysteria, whether she is telling a funny story or remembering the terrible last days at Belle Reve, and this is what gives the play its dramatic tension. From our first meeting with Blanche we sense the potential for tragedy in this slight, dainty figure. It should be stressed, however, that Blanche makes no blatant bids for our sympathy. Williams makes her a constant irritant in the Kowalski household with her artificial gaiety, her snobbery, her determination to impose her character on the apartment and her private jokes at Mitch's expense. (See, for instance, the scene in which she suggests they pretend they are in Paris, Scene VI, when she propositions him in French, secure in the knowledge that he will not understand her.) She makes her sister run errands for her even when she knows that Stella is pregnant. On the whole she has no regard for her sister's feelings, making no secret of her contempt for Stella's domestic circumstances and for her uncouth Polish husband. As a house guest in a two-room apartment she is obviously a trial, and we experience a sneaking sympathy for Stanley, forever kept out of the bathroom by Blanche's indulgence in hot baths for her nerves. (It is obvious that Williams, as well as using Blanche's baths as a means of raising tension in the household, wishes to stress Blanche's need for a symbolic cleansing to rinse away her sordid past. Her mania for cleanliness is stressed over and over again, especially in the final scene when, bathed and clean, she asks anxiously whether the grapes have been washed and dreams of being buried at sea in a clean white sack.)

When we come to hear the final, true account of her husband's suicide (Scene VI) we learn that he shot himself after she had blurted out publicly her disgust at his homosexuality. She knows, of course, that it was her words that drove him to suicide and the Varsouviana music is the expression of her horror and guilt at that knowledge. (We might consider – as no one in the play seems to – what the effect of catching her husband in bed with a man must have had on a very young and unstable girl).

Stella implies that there had always been some concern in the family over Blanche's behaviour, regarded as 'flighty'. Frankness about sexual matters was not yet the norm, but we may assume that, at least after her husband's death if not before, Blanche's flirtatiousness went beyond the acceptable limits. Certainly in her last years at Laurel she was wildly promiscuous, drinking and sleeping with soldiers, and making at least one attempt to seduce a pupil. The episode with the young man from the *Evening Star* in Scene V is a deliberate repetition of her past behaviour, stressing the reckless streak in her nature as she risks discovery by Mitch. Blanche herself hints obliquely (she always avoids outspokenness in sexual matters) at her understanding for a brief passionate affair ('someone to go out with – once – twice – three times when the devil is in you' – Scene IV). Using the metaphor of the streetcar the sisters speak of sexual passion, and Blanche admits quietly that it was this, desire, that reduced her to having to live on her sister's charity ('Haven't you ever ridden on that street-car?' . . . 'It brought me here' – Scene IV).

Because she lives in our imagination beyond the confines of the play, we wonder how long her marriage to Mitch would have lasted before she broke out either from boredom or because her need for sexual encounters drove her. As she appears completely self-centred it is unlikely that she would have controlled herself out of consideration for her dull, kindly husband. The episode with the young man from the newspaper promises ill for her marital fidelity.

Her vanity is irritating and pathetic in equal parts. We sympathise with Stella when she responds to Blanche's blatant demands for flattery 'a little wearily' and 'dutifully' (Scene I). Her unsuccessful flirtation with Stanley in Scene II is again a bid for flattery and admiration, pitiful because it misfires. In the last scene when Stella reminds Eunice to compliment her sister on her looks and Eunice complies, the effect is to arouse our pity for the ignorant victim's complacency. She is also very conscious of her age, and repeatedly claims to be the younger sister, though she is in fact five years older than Stella. Viewed from our present-day perspective a woman of thirty or thereabouts has hardly reached the age when she has to seek soft lighting to mitigate the ravages of advancing years. At the same time as pretending to be the younger sister, however, she uses her position as the elder sister to make Stella run errands for her, while Stanley watches resentfully.

There is contradiction too between the playful cliché-ridden diction she uses in her flirtations, and her genuine love for poetry, for the language of real emotion. When she makes her drunken boast to Stanley about the 'beauty of the mind and richness of the spirit and tenderness of the heart' (Scene X), she is speaking the truth. She has all these qualities but she also possesses a voracious sexual appetite and it is the conflict of these two aspects of her character that destroys her. She pleads that it was 'panic, just panic, that drove [her] from one to another' (Scene IX), and that seems to be the author's view of her, expressed also in the Hart Crane epigraph ('I entered the broken world/To trace the visionary company of love . . . But not for long to hold each desperate choice'). But again she seems to have become a much more complex character than perhaps her author intended, her sexuality claiming a more dominant part in her make-up than might have been acceptable in the late forties. If it is true that Williams saw in her a coded representation of himself, then it might reasonably be suggested that he saw himself, like his heroine, by the soft, romantic light of her Chinese lantern.

Stanley Kowalski

As a dramatic character Stanley is a well-rounded creation, though he does not exercise our imagination in the same way as Blanche. He has no life outside the play, though we may wonder a little about the future of his marriage. Do Eunice and Steve with their noisy quarrels and fights foreshadow the Kowalskis' future? Within the play, however, Stanley performs two important functions, always in polarity with Blanche.

First there is the sexual tension between them which Stanley acknowledges openly. In Scene II he responds to Blanche's flirtatious manner by saying 'If I didn't know that you was my wife's sister I'd get ideas about you'. In Scene V he refuses to kiss his wife in front of her sister, thus showing his sexual awareness of Blanche, and in the final confrontation with Blanche in Scene X he declares just before the rape: 'We've had this date with each other from the beginning!' Blanche too is aware of the sexual tension between them, saying to Mitch in Scene VI: 'Of course there is such a thing as the hostility of – perhaps in some perverse kind of way he – No! To think of it makes me . . .'

While acknowledging Stanley's sexual attraction to women ('the only way to live with such a man is to – go to bed with him') Blanche is contemptuous of his coarse animal vitality. She launches into a lengthy and exaggerated description of him as the ape-like caveman in Scene IV, to which Stanley listens unobserved. While she attempts to conceal the sexual tension between them under her verbiage, Stanley has assessed Blanche's ambivalent feelings towards him and despises her all the more for them, both before and after the rape.

His other function is to represent the vigour of the new order as opposed to the effeminacy of the old. He is an immigrant, proud of being an

American and eager to make his way in this promised land. As he sees it, it is a land in which there is no place for the old order of the Southern aristocracy who are incapable of holding on to their inherited wealth. A comparison has been made with August Strindberg's *Miss Julie*, and it is a legitimate one, especially if we remember Williams's thorough knowledge of the work of the Swedish playwright, going back to his years at the University of Missouri. Miss Julie's affair with the coarse valet, Jean, offers some parallels with *A Streetcar Named Desire*, in the characters of the protagonists and to a certain extent in the nature of their relationship. Another parallel may legitimately be drawn with D. H. Lawrence's Lady Chatterley and Mellors, the gamekeeper, especially if we recall Williams's profound admiration for Lawrence.

The contrast between Blanche and Stanley is also cultural; where she stands for spiritual values and a literary heritage he is lodged in the factual (we note his obsession with the 'Napoleonic Code') and the physical. He sees Blanche's pretensions and fantasies as contemptible ('lies and conceit and tricks' – Scene X), and is quite incapable of understanding that she needs them to reassure herself, not to impress others. He has no pity for her and apparently suffers no remorse for his vile act: raping his wife's sister (and so breaking an ancient taboo) while his wife is giving birth to his child seems to him quite excusable because according to his moral code she asked for it. In Williams's day the term 'machismo' had not yet gained currency, but surely Stanley is the prototype of the macho man. He has a set of standards to which he adheres but they apply to men only. Thus he betrays Blanche's past to Mitch because his conscience will not allow him to let his friend be caught by her lies. His love for his wife is a powerful sexual passion which binds them both. The only tenderness of which he is capable is within their sexual relationship.

Though uneducated he is no fool; in fact our attention is drawn repeatedly to his shrewdness. Quite early in the play he makes a laconic comment on the half-empty whisky bottle ('Liquor goes fast in hot weather' – Scene I), and we feel sure that he has guessed who had drunk it. Driven by his dislike of her he has ferreted out Blanche's past skilfully, while remaining quite unable to grasp the hidden causes of her behaviour. In dramatic terms Blanche's condemnation of his character which he overhears in Scene IV is as much of a spur to investigate her history as the sexual antagonism between them. Perhaps his habit of classifying women sexually has also alerted him to the other side of Blanche's character, making him wary of her protestations of gentility.

Despite his force and vitality, Stanley does at times appear to be foolish and lacking in judgment, as in his misguided insistence on the relevance of the Napoleonic Code to his claims on Stella's inheritance, or in his naïve overestimation of the value of Blanche's costume jewellery and furs. His male friends all acknowledge his leadership, but given the sort of men they are this is not greatly to his credit: he is the biggest fish in a very small pond.

Much has been made of Stanley's machismo as perceived by the homosexual Williams. The playwright certainly had much difficulty in creating Stanley's character, which changed in the various different versions of the play. In the earliest version he is of Italian origin, a playful, tender weakling. In a later version he is Irish and the feminine streak in his character is very much stressed, making his relationship with his sister-in-law much more complex. In the final version Williams revised Stanley's character drastically, making him the opposite to Blanche in every way, her antagonist. In dramatic terms this transformation works; in terms of the playwright's empathies with his characters it represents a radical shift. Williams has no sympathy for Stanley, 'the gaudy seed-bearer', and this affects his handling of Stanley's part in the play. Remember, for instance, the small physical detail of his protruding tongue as he approaches Blanche in the rape scene, which undoubtedly turns him into the conventional villain.

We know little about his past and are not encouraged to speculate about his future. The part demands an actor with a considerable physical magnetism (such as Marlon Brando had when he played Stanley on the stage and, later, on the screen), because the physical qualities of the character are stressed so much: his sexuality, his relish of rich food, his pleasure in his sporting ability, the joy of living which he exudes. His thoughts, however, remain largely his own, except for his pride in his American citizenship and his touchiness about his humble Polish origins, both of which serve to emphasise the vast difference in social background between him and the sisters. No doubt his wife's social superiority plays a part in their relationship which he sees as an exercise of power: by making love to her he has pulled Stella off the colonnade of her ancestral mansion ('I pulled you down off them columns and how you loved it' – Scene VIII). Perhaps it is not such a long step from seeing the sexual act as an assertion of superiority to making it the instrument of humiliation in a rape.

In the tragic last scene Stanley's part is almost passive: he carries on with the card game as an act of bravado, but at the moment of crisis, with Blanche struggling to break free from the Matron, we find Stanley calling to the Doctor for help. His hold over his friends has weakened, perhaps temporarily, but his future position seems of no interest. He has been dismissed by the author, having played his part as the destroyer of Blanche's mind.

Stella Kowalski

At first glance so passive, so submissive as to have almost no character of her own, Stella grows into a very intriguing person. First of all, we are

never told exactly why she had so resolutely turned her back on Belle
Reve: did she see the writing on the wall, and decide to save herself from
the coming ruin? Or was she simply tired of living in her flamboyant
sister's shadow? ('I just got in the habit of being quiet around you', she
says to Blanche in Scene I). We do not know what she did after she left
Belle Reve, we do not even know how old she was when she left. There
never was a complete rift, as the sisters corresponded, and apparently
Stella went back for the funerals of the elderly relatives ('You just came
home in time for the funerals' – Scene I). The one thing we are certain
about is her passionate attachment to Stanley, to which she confesses
openly and movingly in Scene I ('And when he comes back I cry on his
lap like a baby'). Strong sexuality is a characteristic both sisters share;
both sisters know all about 'that rattle-trap streetcar' (Scene IV), but
whereas Blanche, for the most part, denies her feelings, Stella acknowledges hers and focuses them on one man only.

Stanley reminds Stella that she thought him common when they first
met (and for him the thought that she was so superior to him socially
was an added attraction). By this time, however, she sees her husband
differently and feels sure of his ability to prosper in life. Moreover, as we
are told indirectly, she has learnt to accept his values – she enjoys watch-
ing him play bowls with his mates, and when she is resting, she reads a
comic, not a book. At the same time, when she is with her sister, she
reverts to some of her old attitudes, and she and Blanche enjoy making
fun of the vulgar wives of Stanley's friends ('with girlish laughter', as
Williams puts it rather snidely). She and Stanley are amused by the noisy
quarrels between Eunice and Steve, and their tolerant amusement arises
out of the background they now share. (We might wonder whether the
figure of the fat, jealous Eunice hints at what Stella might be like one day,
blowsy and fat after too many pregnancies.)

Underneath her apparent passivity there is hard determination and this is
recognised by Blanche in Scene I when she says to her sister 'I never had
your beautiful self-control'. Stella will not leave her husband and will go
to any lengths to keep her marriage. This is shown plainly in the last scene
where she weeps for her sister, but only after she has admitted openly
that she refuses to accept her sister's story of the rape, because if she
believed that Blanche was telling the truth, she could not go on living with
Stanley. This she is not prepared to do, and she has therefore accepted that
Blanche's version of the events is the fabrication of a sick mind. The direct
result of this is, of course, Blanche's commital to a mental hospital (an act
of treachery that naturally reverberated in Williams's own mind, for not
only did his mother betray Rose in the same way but he was in part guilty
of the same treason by default).

Stella is presented with a choice: the world of Belle Reve against New
Orleans, Blanche against Stanley. The outcome is not entirely predictable:

Blanche's hold over her sister rests on shared memories, shared values (which Stella is trying to discard), and the influence of the older sister over the younger one. Blanche plays on this, unconsciously perhaps, forcing Stella back into the role of the baby sister ('You messy child' in Scene I, 'Baby, my baby sister!' in Scene IV), and seeing herself as Stella's protectress against the drunken Stanley. At this point the cool, rational side of Stella's nature (which led her to leave Belle Reve) takes over, and Blanche's histrionics on the morning after the poker party finally settle the matter. There is no future for her in joining her sister in a life of material insecurity and fantasies of a better future. Not uncritical of Stanley's shortcomings, Stella still decides that her future lies with him, and so she seals Blanche's fate.

Mitch

The last of the foursome, Mitch's part in the play is first of all as a foil to Stanley. Gentle, conventional, happy to cherish the memory of a dead girl and remain his mother's loving son at home, he is everything that Stanley is not. His manner of speaking is markedly different from the ungrammatical, coarse Stanley: notice how he refers politely to perspiration, refusing to take off his coat because he is sweating, while Stanley speaks frankly of sweat and takes off not only his jacket but his braces and shirt as well.

Mitch is deliberately made out to be a slightly comic figure, mocked by his mates, by Blanche, and even by the playwright himself who describes him as moving to the waltz on Blanche's radio *'in awkward imitation like a dancing bear'* (Scene III). Alone with Blanche he cuts a sorry figure, his dull, cliché-ridden conversation contrasting with the flights of her fancy. When she describes the Pleiades as ladies on their way home from a bridge party, he listens, embarrassed and uncomprehending. He is fascinated by Blanche's delicate beauty, her ladylike ways, her love of poetry, and she plays up to him, half-mockingly acting out his image of herself.

Yet she is aware of his decency and kindness, and responds to it with honesty. It is Mitch who hears the truth about the end of her marriage, and draws her towards him. As she says later, in Scene IX, 'I thanked God for you, because you seemed to be gentle'. His solidity and honesty make her earlier mockery of him in Scene VI seem cheap. He is shattered when he learns of Blanche's past, and shocked into harshness. When he rips off the paper lantern over the light bulb, it is an act of deliberate cruelty, carried out in order to cause her pain. His drunken attempt to rape her in Scene IX is a failure, and he runs off, easily repulsed by a hint of public scandal.

The final irony is that the rape in which he failed is carried out by the man he has looked up to. When he shatters her hopes of peace and safety in marriage, Blanche becomes the crushed victim, her weakness inviting

Stanley's brutality. Herein lies Mitch's second function in the play, to be the unwitting instrument of Blanche's destruction. In the final scene his inarticulate grief has a dignity which Stanley's blustering lacks, and Mitch becomes Stanley's foil yet again, offering a contrast to Stanley's casual brutality.

The literary background

The literature of the American South

Although Williams's first successful play, *The Glass Menagerie*, opened in New York a few months before the end of the Second World War, we find no reflection of the momentous events of the preceding years in his work. The historical events that might be said to have affected him are those of some eighty years before, when the South was defeated in the American Civil War (1861–5), thus failing to secede from the Union in a bid to preserve the slavery system on which its whole thriving economy was based.

The literature of the American South, confidently predicted to be doomed to extinction after the Civil War, revived and continued to thrive on nostalgia, on regional patriotism, and on the peculiar appeal of a lost cause. There is a parallel to be drawn here with the Jacobite cause in Scotland, which inspired some of Sir Walter Scott's best novels, and two small masterpieces by R. L. Stevenson (*Kidnapped* and *Catriona*). It is imperative that the cause should be lost, and that a whole national culture should be endangered, before a writer's imagination can set to work.

In the American South, as well as lamenting a lost cause, many writers defended the indefensible – the slavery of the tobacco and cotton fields – as a way to counter the harsh materialism of the industrial North. This regionalism, unrealistic in many ways, proved as popular in the North as in the South: the gleaming porticoed mansions of the planters, the beauty of the Southern belles, and the suffering of the enslaved blacks, were all irresistibly romantic subjects. The need to record, often in an idealised form, what was passing away for good, was very strong.

Gradually the romanticising impulse weakened, to be revived once more in the famous 1936 bestseller by Margaret Mitchell, *Gone with the Wind*, and in its even more famous film version. New writers came forward, whose Southern-ness was an innate part of their nature, not a flag-waving cause. Among the critics H. L. Mencken (1880–1935), Robert Penn Warren (*b*. 1905) and Cleanth Brooks (*b*. 1906) are all Southerners, Penn Warren being also a novelist of note, the author of *All the King's Men* (1946). Some of the best American novelists of this century came from the South: Thomas Wolfe (1900–38), the author of *Look Homeward, Angel* (1929), came from North Carolina. William Faulkner (1897–1962), who created in an imaginary county, Yoknapatawpha, a complex history of the South, came, like Williams, from Mississippi. Georgia produced Erskine Caldwell (b. 1903), the author of *Tobacco Road* (1932) and *God's Little Acre* (1933), and Carson McCullers (1917–67), the author of *The Heart is a Lonely Hunter* (1940), *Reflections in a Golden Eye* (1941) and *The Member of the Wedding* (1946).

What writers like Faulkner and McCullers shared was an awareness of a dying culture reflected in its members. The romantic mansions were decaying now, and the people who engaged these writers' interest were the lonely, the mis-shapen, the doomed, the outsiders. The sense of an inbred culture is very strong in their work, and this is what links Williams to both Faulkner and McCullers (who was a personal friend of his right up to her death). Most of Williams's plays have a Southern background. Although his attitude to the romanticised Old South was adversely affected by his antipathy to his mother, a professional Southern belle so to speak, one aspect of the Southern culture had an immediate appeal for him. The eccentric, the outcast flourished there, and his Blanche DuBois and the Wingfields of *The Glass Menagerie* were at home there.

American post-war drama

Williams's plays, though they outwardly remain realistic in their settings, are concerned with matters that reach beyond any historical period. The nostalgia for the Old South becomes simply an obsession, which could easily take another form altogether and still remain dramatically valid. Gradually he moved beyond the confines of realism altogether, as his melodramatic plots demanded characters that no longer belonged to a realistic drama. The term 'Southern Gothic', used to describe the excessive, sensational aspect of Southern literature, applies well to Williams.

He offers an interesting contrast to the other two American playwrights who appeared on the literary scene at about the same time: Arthur Miller (b. 1915) and Edward Albee (b. 1928). Miller's *All My Sons* was staged in 1947, his *Death of a Salesman* in 1949, followed by *The Crucible* in 1953 and *After the Fall* in 1964. The settings are realistic, but the plays are ultimately concerned not with reality but with moral problems of universal, timeless validity – dishonesty, moral cowardice, political oppression (*The Crucible* being a fable of the McCarthy anti-Communist inquisitions). Where Williams turns to sensationalist subjects that satisfy both his dramatic urge and his desire to express his personal isolation from society, Miller turns to drama as a vehicle for thought. His political allegiance is to the left, and though his plays are not in any way political propaganda, his sense of moral outrage is often based on contemporary issues.

The third writer, Edward Albee, is in some ways closer to Williams, notably in his predilection for the bizarre. *Zoo Story* (1959) centres on a young drifter's death wish, while *The American Drama* (1961) has for its subject the parents' murder of an unsatisfactory child, and *The Death of Bessie Smith* (1961) deals with the notorious circumstances of the death of the famous black jazz singer. Albee's best-known play is *Who's Afraid of Virginia Woolf?* (1962), an analysis of an unhappy marriage in a form that both shocked and mesmerised the audiences. A later play, *A Delicate Balance*, deals with madness, a subject that stresses his affinities with Williams, though for Albee the sensational elements are ultimately symbols, the means to an end.

Mention should also be made here of William Inge (1913–73), one-time friend and rival of Williams, whose play *Come Back, Little Sheba* was, like a number of Williams's plays, a success on the stage and as a film. Like Williams, too, Inge became dependent on alcohol and drugs and after several failed suicide attempts he finally succeeded in killing himself.

Though Miller is still writing (his latest play *Broken Glass* finds inspiration in the *Kristallnacht*, the infamous anti-semitic demonstrations in Nazi Germany), and Albee has recently been awarded the Pulitzer Prize for his play *Three Tall Women*, American drama has now moved beyond self-examination and preoccupation with moral problems. Arthur Kopit's (*b.* 1937) *Oh Dad, Poor Dad, Mamma's Hung You in the Closet and I'm Feeling So Sad* (1966) is a farce, and his *Indians* (1968) a presentation of the dark side of American history. Sam Shepherd's (*b.* 1943) short plays, *Five Plays* (1967), for instance, or *Fool for Love*, employ his undisciplined imagination in satirising the United States of today. David Mamet (*b.* 1947) is perhaps the most successful as well as the most varied of the new dramatists. His *American Buffalo* came out in 1977, to be followed by a savage satire on the real estate business, *Glengarry Glen Ross* (1984), and most recently by *Oleanna* (1992), a controversial attack on feminism and on the issues surrounding sexual harassment.

What these new writers have in common is perhaps, that while taking some form of moral stand, they lack *gravitas*, asserting instead, by implication at least, that all life is a farce. Williams had played his part in the development of post-war American drama, only to be left behind.

Part 4

Hints for study

Reading the play

At first glance it may seem easier to choose a play as the subject of your study rather than a novel. But though the text will certainly be much shorter, the careful study of a play is hard work, and you will have to use your imagination much more. After all, in a novel the author provides descriptions of the appearance, and of mental and moral qualities of each character, as well as of the background of the action, in addition to usually quite plentiful dialogues. His authorial voice too is often heard, offering opinions and passing judgments.

The readers of a play, by contrast, have little to guide them other than the conversations between the characters and the stage directions describing their movements on the stage. There will be some descriptions of the physical appearance of the characters, in modern plays at least. (Notice the almost complete absence of any descriptions of people or settings in earlier drama, including Shakespeare, and notice also how little you miss them. The playwright provides any descriptions needed in the speeches of the characters.) There will also be stage directions, varying in length and detail from playwright to playwright. (Of the dramatists of the present age, George Bernard Shaw offers copious entertaining descriptions, Samuel Beckett almost none, while both Ibsen and Chekhov, characteristically, describe the sets in factual, realistic detail, leaving the characters to our imagination.) Tennessee Williams's descriptions of both people and settings are quite detailed, and include evocative sketches not only of the main characters' appearance but of their qualities as well: remember the detailed description of Stanley, as *'the gaudy seed-bearer'*, which seems to betray a certain antagonism on the playwright's part.

When discussing a play, you will be expected to form your own opinions of the characters and their actions and motives, rather than repeating the playwright's summaries. No-one will expect you to accept the characters at their author's or critics' valuation; indeed you may find it easier and more interesting to disagree, as long as you can support your arguments by accurate references to the play, based on a careful reading. This is where your imagination comes into play, literally. You will have to visualise the action on the stage, hear in your mind the actors' voices, and very often decide on the tone in which they speak their lines. It is recommended to the students of a play to make every effort to see a stage performance of it or a screen version (which may well be available on video). It is certainly the easiest and most natural way of getting to know the play, but of course you will then unconsciously accept the values and interpretations of that particular production, and may find it much more difficult to form your own independent judgment. Thus those who have seen the famous Elia Kazan film of *A Streetcar Named Desire*, with Vivien Leigh and Marlon Brando in the leading roles, will find it impossible for quite some time afterwards not to rerun the film in their minds.

Having to rely on the text alone has some advantages and what you write down as the result of your work will be entirely your own impressions and thoughts. However, you will have to make sure that you acquire a thorough, detailed knowledge of the text and the first step is of course to read the play right through, just to get the flavour and feel of it. You do not need to take notes at this stage, though you may find that you want to jot down your ideas as you go. (Remember to write down enough to identify the passage, with a page reference to the text of the play. Hours can be wasted in trying to track down an imperfectly remembered passage.) During your second reading you would be well advised to take detailed notes, separately for each scene. (It may sound quite alarming that you should read and reread the play at a time when you are under pressure, but the comparatively short length of the play works in your favour.) The 'detailed summaries' of Part 2 of these Notes will help you, but if you can, write down your own versions of these summaries. They will then reflect your own viewpoint and emphasise what you yourself find most important in each scene. Writing down the summaries will also help you to clarify the sequence of events in your mind.

If there are several of you who have chosen to study the same play, you might find it useful to do a joint play-reading, with different people taking the main parts in turn. (Needless to say, this will be a complete waste of time if you treat the play-reading as a joke. It is difficult not to feel self-conscious during this exercise, but you might find it useful to remember its purpose.) One of the benefits of a play-reading is that it enables you to hear the characters' reactions to one another, to see the play as action rather than a sequence of speeches. If you are reading the play by yourself, even if you are reading it aloud (as you should), you are still hearing only your own voice, and you may miss some of the dramatic interactions. Therefore, if you have to study entirely on your own, do take the trouble to read the play slowly and to think of it as a movement forward. The play has its own momentum, and the author is at pains repeatedly to mark its progress towards the final catastrophe. A careful reading will reward you by drawing your attention to these markers (such as for instance some of Stanley's remarks to Blanche during their first meeting). Repetitions too have their own significance, either to stress the importance of what is being said, or, by varying the wording and content to elaborate an earlier statement further. (Blanche's gradual revelation of the truth about her marriage is a case in point. Her prevarications serve to heighten the impact of the final, true account in Scene VI.)

Preparing for an examination

It is important that you should know the play really well, scene by scene, so that you can refer to incidents in the play with confidence, identifying correctly the scene in which they occur. If you have your own notes on the scenes one by one, read them over to see if they include what your careful study tells you are the crucial incidents. Test the usefulness of your notes by identifying in your mind the incidents that you are likely to refer to in any essay you write. Set them down as headings: 'Blanche's marriage' would be one such heading, obviously, under which you would list her references to her tragic marriage in Scenes I, III and IX, Stella's version of the facts in Scene VII, as well as the fact that the two sisters never speak of it to one another. In this way you will make sure that you know the play really well, and that you will be able to use this knowledge to support your arguments in your essay. Rather than memorising lengthy quotations, it is easier to remember the rough outline of each scene so as to refer to an incident correctly by the scene in which it occurs.

If you wish to quote the text in your essay, be sure that you quote accurately. This is not easy, especially when you are writing under stress during an examination, so do try to keep your quotations short and limit them in number. The following quotations are examples which you may find useful: Blanche in Scene I: 'Funerals are quiet, but deaths – not always'; in Scene V: 'the soft people have got to – shimmer and glow – put a – paper lantern over the light' and, speaking to the young man in the same scene: 'You make my mouth water'; in Scene XI: 'buried at sea sewn up in a clean white sack' and 'I have always depended on the kindness of strangers'; Stanley in Scene VIII: 'how you loved it, having them coloured lights going!' and in Scene X: 'We've had this date with each other from the beginning!'

Gradually, as you get to know the play well, you will become clearer in your mind as to which aspects of it appeal to you most. If at this stage you cast your eye over the specimen questions on page 69, you can decide which of them you would find the easiest and most congenial to answer. This will tell you which would be the most profitable line of study for you to pursue. It may be a discussion of the characters. In that case, think how you would deal with a question of that kind, consider which incidents are the most illuminating for the character under discussion, and test your knowledge of the play by listing these incidents and the scenes in which they occur. The list of specimen questions is obviously not an exhaustive one, and you should be able to think of other themes for discussion.

If a question stimulates your interest, sketch out briefly in your mind (or on a piece of paper) the form your answer would take. This is another useful exercise: you may well find that as you try to tackle a question that seemed challenging you soon run out of ideas and your arguments do not stand up. If you are to deal with a question to your own (and the examiner's) satisfaction, transitory interest – which may be no more than a chance to use a favourite quotation – is not enough. You must have enough ideas to sustain an essay of a reasonable length. Once you have chosen a question that appeals to you, you should test yourself by answering it under examination conditions. You cannot, of course, reproduce the strain of sitting an examination, but you can set yourself a time within which to answer the question. A study of earlier examination papers will tell you how many questions you will be expected to answer within the allotted time, and how much time you will have for each of them. Settle on the time you will allow yourself for one question, but remember that in the examination you will need to allow extra time for studying the unfamiliar examination paper and choosing the questions to answer. You should also allow time for reading over your essay at the end, to fill in any missing words or correct any spelling mistakes that might have crept in. Having worked out the time allowed, start on your essay. Jot down the line of your arguments, check that they actually form an answer to the question, arrange them in logical order, and start writing. As you write, keep glancing back at your notes as well as the actual question, to make sure you have not strayed from the line you are proposing to take to answer the question. It is wiser not to change your argument once you have started, because if you alter your approach radically, you are unlikely to finish in time.

Though the examiners will not expect a polished piece of prose, it is sensible to start with an introduction outlining your arguments roughly. Follow it up with a discussion, point by point, keeping to the order of your introductory outline. Close with a summing up in which you repeat the salient points of your argument. Read your essay over carefully, checking the spelling as well as any quotations or references to the text of the play. All this time keep firmly before you the question you are supposed to answer in your essay. When you have finished, consider carefully the time you took over the essay. If you have overrun your allotted time badly, you will need to reconsider your examination strategy and try to be more concise in your answer. Indeed, if you have any time to spare at all, you will find practising to answer questions within a time limit an invaluable aid. If time allows, it might also be useful at this stage to read one or two other plays by Williams, *The Glass Menagerie* in particular. You will find the comparison with *A Streetcar Named Desire* interesting and illuminating. There is a world of difference between thinking about a question, and actually putting your thoughts down on paper and shaping them into an essay. It is a far more disciplined effort, and one that does not come easily.

at the start of the play he describes this music as
the life' of New Orleans, and certainly throughout
...ic increases significantly in volume at moments of
... It is a life-asserting voice, and so is heard almost
...anche tells of the loss of Belle Reve (a symbol of
... in Scene I, and again in Scene II when she hears of

...when the people of the quarter go about their pleasures,
...g, making love. Thus, significantly, the play closes with
..., as Stanley's love-making enables Stella to forget her
...wn guilt.
...asure in the _'blue piano'_, but no sweetness, no compassion;
...are reminded that the vitality of New Orleans can also turn
...Thus in Scene X just before the rape the music of the _'blue_
...into inhuman jungle-like cries (in popular imagination jazz
...ted with Africa, with tribal music in the jungle).
...ond musical voice in the play is the _'Varsouviana'_ polka, a
...of the scene on the ballroom floor when Blanche publicly
...d her husband and so drove him to suicide. It is made very clear
...dience that Blanche is the only person to hear this tune, and that it
...ends with the sound of a shot. She waits for this sound, to put an
...the unbearable reminder of past tragedy. It is, however, not just a
...cal memory of her husband's suicide. It also acts as a dark warning of
...ster about to strike. Thus it accompanies Stanley's cruel birthday
...sent to Blanche of a bus ticket back to Laurel (Scene VIII); it is played
...ain as Blanche, drunk and despairing, sits alone in the apartment just
...efore Mitch arrives to revile her, and it comes and goes throughout the
...ragic last scene.

The polka tune is more specific than the _'blue piano'_, as it is heard only
by Blanche, and only in response to her particular situation. Nevertheless
both tunes share one significant characteristic: they are in no sense background music only and have an important dramatic function in the play.
This function is either to underline an existing situation (this might be said
particularly of the _'blue piano'_), or to act as an alarm, a warning, as well
as the evocation of a tragic memory (the _'Varsouviana'_). Such a use of
music may well have been inspired by the cinema, where music is used a
great deal. However, Williams's use of music is far more deliberate and
specific, than that which is generally found in films and might also be said
to represent the clash of two societies, the new, mixed-race New Orleans
and the dying old South. These distinctive tunes are voices without words,
and we should listen to them carefully as they speak their parts in the play.

Practice will not make ~~~
confidence as well.

Specimen

(1) The America~~~
lack of coheren~~~
theatre, [a] sentin~~~
ported by any basic~~~
(2) Do you think that the~~~
the play, or could the a~~~
altogether?
(3) Is Mitch simply a foil to St~~~
of his own in the play?
(4) Discuss the role of music in *A* ~~~
(5) Does Williams intend Blanche t~~~
so, does he succeed in this?
(6) Do you think *A Streetcar Named D*~~~
ventional three-act play, and how woul~~~
(7) Is *A Streetcar Named Desire* a play to~~~
stage?
(8) Which of the relationships between the c~~~
Named Desire develop in the course of the p~~~
the same, and why?
(9) Blanche and Stanley are certainly the two main ch~~~
Whom do you see as the third most important person~~~
(10) Williams saw himself as a lyrical writer. Do you ~~~
estimation of his own talent?

Specimen answer

(4) Discuss the role of a music in *A Streetcar Named Desire*

There are two distinctive kinds of music in the play, and it is obvious from.
the stage directions that Tennessee Williams attached considerable importance to them both.

The first is the music of the *'blue piano'*, a term devised by Williams to
describe the blues music, which had it origins in the passionate songs of
the Southern blacks. In New Orleans it evolved into a sophisticated
musical form, primarily associated with the bars and night clubs of the
city. As for Williams himself New Orleans had been the city of his artistic
and sexual liberation, so the *'blue piano'* (and trumpet, drum and
saxophone) are to him voices of unrestrained physical pleasure, at times
menacing in their animal strength and abandon, but always full of vitality.

In the stage directions~~~
expressing *'the spirit o*~~~
the play the piano mu~~~
dramatic importance~~~
in triumph when Bl~~~
Southern decadence~~~
Stella's pregnancy.
We hear it also~~~
drinking, laughin~~~
the *'blue piano*~~~
sister and her o~~~
There is ple~~~
through it we~~~
ugly, violent~~~
piano' turns~~~
was associa~~~
The se~~~
reminder~~~
renounc~~~
to the a~~~
always~~~
end t~~~
musi~~~
disa~~~
pre~~~
ag~~~
b~~~
t~~~

interesting, especially in what Mrs Williams does not choose to mention.

WINDHAM, DONALD: *Tennessee Williams' Letters to Donald Windham, 1940–65*, Holt, Rinehart & Winston, New York, 1977. The record of a long-lasting friendship, of literary as well as personal interest.

Criticism

FALK, SIGNI: *Tennessee Williams*, Twayne Publishers, New York, 1961. A critical discussion of Williams's plays, with detailed summaries of the plots.

LEAVITT, RICHARD (ED.): *The World of Tennessee Williams*, G. P. Putnam's Sons, New York, 1978. A collection of occasional writings etc.

McCANN, JOHN S.: *The Critical Reputation of Tennessee Williams*, G. K. Hall, Boston, Massachusetts, 1983.

STANTON, STEPHEN S. (ED.): *Tennessee Williams: A Collection of Critical Essays*, Prentice-Hall, Englewood Cliffs, New Jersey, 1977.

Bibliography

GUNN, D. W.: *Tennessee Williams: A Bibliography*, Scarecrow Press, Metuchen, New Jersey and London, 1980.

The author of these notes

HANA SAMBROOK was educated at the Charles University in Prague and at the University of Edinburgh. She worked for some years in Scottish educational publishing, and was later on the staff of the Edinburgh University Library. Now a freelance editor in London, she is the author of the York Notes on *The Tenant of Wildfell Hall, Lark Rise to Candleford, Victory, My Family and Other Animals, Selected Works of Sylvia Plath*, and *I'm the King of the Castle*.

Part 5

Suggestions for further reading

The text

A Streetcar Named Desire. With commentary and notes by Patricia Hern, Methuen, London, 1984 (Methuen Student Edition), reprinted in 1994. This is the edition used in the preparation of these Notes.

Sweet Bird of Youth. A Streetcar Named Desire. The Glass Menagerie, Penguin Books, Harmondsworth, 1962 (Penguin Twentieth Century Classics).

Other works by Tennessee Williams

Cat on a Hot Tin Roof. The Milk Train Doesn't Stop Here Any More. The Night of the Iguana, Penguin Books, Harmondsworth, 1976 (Penguin Twentieth Century Classics).

Memoirs, Doubleday, Garden City, New York, 1975.

Biographies

HAYMAN, RONALD: *Tennessee Williams: Everyone Else is an Audience*, Yale University Press, New York and London, 1993. A well-written biography, amply furnished with quotations from Williams himself and his friends.

SMITH, BRUCE: *Costly Performances: Tennessee Williams – The Last Stage*, Paragon House, New York, 1990. Recollections by one of the friends of Williams's last years, revealing in more ways than the author perhaps intended.

SPOTO, DONALD: *The Kindness of Strangers: The Life of Tennessee Williams*, Bodley Head, London, 1985. Crammed with painstakingly collected facts, but still readable.

TISCHLER, NANCY M.: *Tennessee Williams: Rebellious Puritan*, The Citadel Press, New York, 1961. A pedestrian biography with emphasis on Williams as a writer.

WILLIAMS, EDWINA DAKIN: *Remember Me to Tom*, G. P. Putnam's Sons, New York, 1963; Cassell, London, 1964. Mrs Williams's memories, ghosted by Lucy Freeman. Though the style is dull, the matter is

Practice will not make perfect, but it certainly helps, and will boost your confidence as well.

Specimen questions

(1) The American novelist Louis Auchincloss said that there was 'a lack of coherent thinking [that] wrought havoc with Williams's later theatre, [a] sentimentality that ultimately broke through walls unsupported by any basic moral fabric'. Do you agree?

(2) Do you think that the Southern American background is essential to the play, or could the action take place against a different background altogether?

(3) Is Mitch simply a foil to Stanley, or does he have a dramatic function of his own in the play?

(4) Discuss the role of music in *A Streetcar Named Desire*.

(5) Does Williams intend Blanche to be a sympathetic character, and if so, does he succeed in this?

(6) Do you think *A Streetcar Named Desire* could be made into a conventional three-act play, and how would it work?

(7) Is *A Streetcar Named Desire* a play to read or a play to see on the stage?

(8) Which of the relationships between the characters in *A Streetcar Named Desire* develop in the course of the play, and which remain the same, and why?

(9) Blanche and Stanley are certainly the two main characters in the play. Whom do you see as the third most important person in the play?

(10) Williams saw himself as a lyrical writer. Do you agree with his estimation of his own talent?

Specimen answer

(4) Discuss the role of a music in *A Streetcar Named Desire*

There are two distinctive kinds of music in the play, and it is obvious from the stage directions that Tennessee Williams attached considerable importance to them both.

The first is the music of the *'blue piano'*, a term devised by Williams to describe the blues music, which had it origins in the passionate songs of the Southern blacks. In New Orleans it evolved into a sophisticated musical form, primarily associated with the bars and night clubs of the city. As for Williams himself New Orleans had been the city of his artistic and sexual liberation, so the *'blue piano'* (and trumpet, drum and saxophone) are to him voices of unrestrained physical pleasure, at times menacing in their animal strength and abandon, but always full of vitality.

In the stage directions at the start of the play he describes this music as expressing *'the spirit of the life'* of New Orleans, and certainly throughout the play the piano music increases significantly in volume at moments of dramatic importance. It is a life-asserting voice, and so is heard almost in triumph when Blanche tells of the loss of Belle Reve (a symbol of Southern decadence) in Scene I, and again in Scene II when she hears of Stella's pregnancy.

We hear it also when the people of the quarter go about their pleasures, drinking, laughing, making love. Thus, significantly, the play closes with the *'blue piano'*, as Stanley's love-making enables Stella to forget her sister and her own guilt.

There is pleasure in the *'blue piano'*, but no sweetness, no compassion; through it we are reminded that the vitality of New Orleans can also turn ugly, violent. Thus in Scene X just before the rape the music of the *'blue piano'* turns into inhuman jungle-like cries (in popular imagination jazz was associated with Africa, with tribal music in the jungle).

The second musical voice in the play is the *'Varsouviana'* polka, a reminder of the scene on the ballroom floor when Blanche publicly renounced her husband and so drove him to suicide. It is made very clear to the audience that Blanche is the only person to hear this tune, and that it always ends with the sound of a shot. She waits for this sound, to put an end to the unbearable reminder of past tragedy. It is, however, not just a musical memory of her husband's suicide. It also acts as a dark warning of disaster about to strike. Thus it accompanies Stanley's cruel birthday present to Blanche of a bus ticket back to Laurel (Scene VIII); it is played again as Blanche, drunk and despairing, sits alone in the apartment just before Mitch arrives to revile her, and it comes and goes throughout the tragic last scene.

The polka tune is more specific than the *'blue piano'*, as it is heard only by Blanche, and only in response to her particular situation. Nevertheless both tunes share one significant characteristic: they are in no sense background music only and have an important dramatic function in the play. This function is either to underline an existing situation (this might be said particularly of the *'blue piano'*), or to act as an alarm, a warning, as well as the evocation of a tragic memory (the *'Varsouviana'*). Such a use of music may well have been inspired by the cinema, where music is used a great deal. However, Williams's use of music is far more deliberate and specific, than that which is generally found in films and might also be said to represent the clash of two societies, the new, mixed-race New Orleans and the dying old South. These distinctive tunes are voices without words, and we should listen to them carefully as they speak their parts in the play.